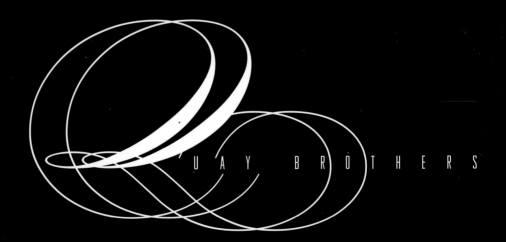

QUAY BROTHERS

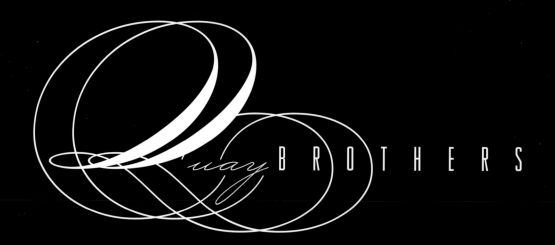

Quay BROTHERS

ON DECIPHERING THE

PHARMACIST'S

PRESCRIPTION FOR LIP-READING

PUPPETS

Ron Magliozzi Edwin Carels

THE
MUSEUM
OF
MODERN
ART

NEW
YORK

Published in conjunction with the exhibition *Quay Brothers: On Deciphering the Pharmacist's Prescription for Lip-Reading Puppets*, at The Museum of Modern Art, New York (August 12, 2012–January 7, 2013), organized by Ron Magliozzi, Associate Curator, Department of Film.

Major support for the exhibition is provided by MoMA's Wallis Annenberg Fund for Innovation in Contemporary Art through the Annenberg Foundation.

Produced by the Department of Publications, The Museum of Modern Art, New York

Edited by Susan Delson

Designed by Roy Brooks, Fold Four, Inc. The cover, the title pages, and the two artists' projects were designed by the Quay Brothers.

Production by Marc Sapir
Color separations by Evergreen Colour Separation (International) Co. Ltd., Hong Kong
Printed and bound by OGI/1010 Printing Group Ltd., China

This book is typeset in Bodoni, Copper, Didot Display, P22 Zaner, Raleigh Gothic, Gill Sans MT, ITC Cheltenham, and Kabel. The paper is 157 gsm Japanese White-A matte Artpaper.

Published by The Museum of Modern Art, 11 W. 53 Street, New York, New York 10019

© 2012 The Museum of Modern Art, New York

Library of Congress Control Number: 2012936892
ISBN: 978-0-87070-843-5

Distributed in the United States and Canada by D.A.P./Distributed Art Publishers, Inc., New York
Distributed outside the United States and Canada by Thames & Hudson Ltd, London

Front cover: *Street of Crocodiles*. 1986. UK. Film: 35mm, color, sound, 20 minutes
Front flap: *Chateau de Labonnécuyère*. c. 1970s. US. Pencil on paper, 28 ⅜ × 18 ½" (27 × 47 cm). QBFZ Collection. See p. 59
Inside front cover and flap, above: on the set of *Institute Benjamenta, or This Dream People Call Human Life*, 1995. Below, left to right: on the set of *The Eternal Day of Michel de Ghelderode, 1898–1962*, 1981; on the set of *The Comb [From the Museums of Sleep]*, 1990.

Back cover: Quay Brothers, c. 1985
Back flap: *Gégène-Le-Joyeux*. c. 1970s. US. Pencil on paper, 13 × 9 ⁷⁄₁₆" (33 × 24 cm). QBFZ Collection. See p. 61
Inside back cover and flap, left: *Ceux Qui Désirent Sans Fin*. c. 1970s. US. Pencil on paper, 11 × 9 ¹⁄₁₆" (28 × 23 cm). QBFZ Collection. Right: *Lover Practicing Hate*. c. 1970s. US. Pencil on paper, 30 ⁵⁄₁₆ × 20 ¹⁄₁₆" (77 × 51 cm). QBFZ Collection. See p. 60

Printed and bound in China

CONTENTS

The book also contains a project by the Quay Brothers on the front and back inside covers.

FOREWORD

The Quay Brothers made their first professional film, the auspicious puppet animation *Nocturna Artificialia*, in 1979. They went on to explore their taste for performance art, object animation, optical phenomena, and obscure biography in a series of experimental documentaries and dark literary adaptations before producing the career-making, stop-motion masterwork *Street of Crocodiles* in 1986. In less than ten years' time the identical twins, born and raised in rural Pennsylvania, had become internationally recognized moving-image artists—enigmatic masters with an Eastern European sensibility that one critic described as a "Mitteleuropa of the mind." Commentators have suggested that the Quay Brothers channel the art of Edvard Munch, Francis Bacon, and Joseph Cornell, share the cinematic temperament of contemporary filmmakers like David Lynch and Guy Maddin, and demonstrate a talent for both animation and live-action that is comparable to that of the surrealist Czech director Jan Švankmajer and mainstream moviemaker Tim Burton. *Quay Brothers: On Deciphering the Pharmacist's Prescription for Lip-Reading Puppets* should serve to prove such comparisons unnecessary. While the mystifying language of the Quay Brothers' animation may require "lip-reading," the "pharmacist's prescription" (or in this case, the curator's prescription) for better understanding the work presented in this exhibition is the full disclosure of their varied accomplishments across a range of mediums.

Thanks to the artists, the Museum has enjoyed greater access to their personal and creative history than they have previously allowed, from private family collections of photographs and memorabilia to the accumulation of curiosities in their London studio, which yielded evidence of their training and early career as graphic designers in the form of drawings, posters, book covers, and record albums. From their studio archives come long-unseen student films, the records of unrealized projects, and copies of little known moving-image work. Taken together, the display of this material offers museum-goers a first-time opportunity to appreciate the Quay Brothers' cohesive, cross-genre mastery of the cinema, stage, site-specific performance, music video, and installation art—not to mention the witty television commercials that represent their stealthiest forays into the heart of pop culture. The twins further exercised their multitasking skills by actively engaging in the process of exhibition planning with the Museum, during a period in which they were simultaneously at work adapting Béla Bartók and Franz Kafka for live presentation in Manchester and Paris, programming events for the Leeds 2012 Cultural Olympiad, and preparing a feature-length screen adaptation of Bruno Schulz's novel *Sanatorium Under the Sign of the Hourglass*.

The nearly three hundred works on paper, objects, and moving-image pieces featured in our galleries testify to the Quay Brothers' achievements. The exhibition also serves to spotlight their collaborators on these various endeavors, including zealous producer Keith Griffiths, a crucial player throughout their career; editor and sound-master Larry Sider; craftsman-technician Ian Nicholas; choreographers Kim Brandstrup and Will Tuckett; composers and musical artists Leszek Jankowski, Krzysztof Penderecki, Steve Martland, Timothy Nelson, David Thomas, Michael Penn, His Name is Alive, Richard Ayres, Martin Ward, and Peter Gabriel; performers Ralf Ralf; and stage directors Richard Jones, Nicholas Broadhurst, and Simon McBurney. It additionally honors the Quays' sources of literary, musical, graphic, and cinematic inspiration: Bruno Schulz, Robert Walser, Franz Kafka, Emma Hauck, Karlheinz Stockhausen, Leoš Janáček, Igor Stravinsky, Rudolf Freund, Roman Cieslewicz, Franciszek Starowieyski, Jan Lenica, Walerian Borowczyk, Luis Buñuel, Jan Švankmajer, Ladislaw Starewicz, and others.

An exhibition this ambitious, with its accompanying film series, would not be possible without the enthusiastic cooperation of our lenders: the Quay Brothers themselves and their family and friends in the United States, including Andrew and Kathy Quay, Susan Freund Borden, and Lydia and Shirley Hunn; and the Quay Brothers' production and distribution partners: the British Film Institute, Channel 4, Zeitgeist Films, Academy Films, and Believe Media. To them all, we express our sincere thanks.

Glenn D. Lowry
Director, The Museum of Modern Art

ACKNOWLEDGMENTS

We are indebted to the Quay Brothers for the extraordinary access they provided us to their archives and personal history, and for their passionate commitment to the rigors of the exhibition process while also working on a new film and serving as curators for the 2012 Cultural Olympiad in Leeds.

We are also grateful for the honor of working with their all-knowing, longtime friend and producer Keith Griffiths, and for the never-failing assistance of their American troubleshooter Edward Waisnis.

An exhibition as comprehensive as *Quay Brothers: On Deciphering the Pharmacist's Prescription for Lip-Reading Puppets* relies on the goodwill and cooperation of many supporters. We are immensely grateful to Andrew and Kathy Quay; Lydia and Shirley Hunn, Susan Borden, and the family of Rudolf Freund; David Thomas of Ubu Projex; artist George Snow; Emily Russo, Nancy Gerstman, and Adrian Curry of Zeitgeist Films, New York; Mark Whittow Williams, Alan Robert Hopkins, and Lizie Gower at Academy Films, London; Luke Thornton and Chloe Lines at Believe Media, Los Angeles; Heather Stewart, Jane Giles, and Nigel Algar at The British Film Institute, London; Sam Sarowitz and Stanley Oh, Posteritati, New York; Patrick Hoffman and Steve Massa, New York Public Library; Robert Barker, Cornell University; media expert Jim McDonnell; Thomas Röske, Prinzhorn Collection, Heidelberg; Salomè Mangles, Keystone; photographers Keith Paisley, J. Gómez Pallarès, Ray Stevenson, Tom Haartsen, and Karen Mauch; the Museum Boijmans van Beuningen, Rotterdam; Oxygénée Ltd.; The Royal Theater of Toone, Brussels; Derek Brazell and

The Association of Illustrators; The British Broadcasting Corporation; C4 Television; Film4; The Arts Council of England; MTV, Viacom Inc.; British Screen; Image Forum; Arte; Zweites Deutsches Fernsehen; Pandora Productions; MedienBoard; UK Film Council; TFC; and the publishers: Picador, Meulenhoff, Bloomsbury, Macmillan, Vintage Books in affiliation with Random House Group Limited, Overlook Press, Dalkey Archive Press, and *Scientific American*, a division of Nature America, Inc.

Much-appreciated aid came from Quay scholars Suzanne Buchan, Edwin Carels, and David Spolum; from George I. Kirkikis, Elif Rongen-Kaynakci, Geoff Brown, Catherine Surowiec, Martin Humphries, Tom Tierney, Alastair Brutchie, Anne Close, John Fontana, and Rob Bozas; from Robert D. Hicks and Evi Numen of the Mütter Museum; and from professor Paul Watry of Liverpool University and Matthew Clough of Liverpool's Victoria Gallery.

At The Museum of Modern Art, for their enduring faith and encouragement, we thank Director Glenn D. Lowry, Associate Director Kathy Halbreich, Chief Operating Officer James Gara, Senior Deputy Director of Exhibitions Ramona Bannayan, Senior Deputy Director of Curatorial Affairs Peter Reed, Senior Deputy Director of External Affairs Michael Margitich, and Rajendra Roy, the Celeste Bartos Chief Curator of Film.

This exhibition would not have been possible without the involvement of Susan Palamara, Allison Needle, Jeri Moxley, Kathryn Ryan, Rob Jung, Sarah Wood, Rachel Abrams, Jack Siman, Erik Landsberg, Robert Kastler, and Roberto Rivera (Collection Management and Exhibition

Registration); Kim Mitchell, Margaret Doyle, Daniela Stigh, and Sarah Jarvis (Communications); Jim Coddington, Roger Griffith (Conservation); Todd Bishop, Lauren Stakias, Heidi Speckhart, Claire Huddleston (Exhibition Fundraising); Jennifer Cohen, Maria DeMarco Beardsley, Jessica Cash (Exhibition Administration); Jerry Neuner, David Hollely, Michele Arms, Peter Perez, Polly Lai, Cynthia Kramer, Carlos Carcamo, William Ashley, Matt Osiol, and Sean Brown (Exhibition Design and Production); Julia Hoffmann, Ingrid Chou, and Claire Corey (Graphic Design); Christopher Hudson, Kara Kirk, David Frankel, Marc Sapir, Hannah Kim, Carey Gibbons, Amanda Washburn, Maria Marchenkova, catalogue editor Susan Delson, reader Thyrza Goodeve Nichols, and designer Roy Brooks (Publications); Aaron Louis, Charles Kalinowski, Howard Deitch, Mike Gibbons, Lucas Gonzalez, Bjorn Quenemoen, Hayna Garcia, Tal Marks, Steven Warrington, Edmund D'Inzillo, Greg Singer, Zdenek Kriz, Allegra Burnette, David Hart, and Chiara Bernasconi (Information Technology); Zoe Jackson, Victor Samra, and Becky Stokes (Marketing); Jan Postma, Julia Kivitz, and Erik Patton (Finance); Patty Lipshutz, Nancy Adelson, and Henry Lanman (General Counsel); Diana Pulling and Blair Dysenchuk (Office of the Director); Tunji Adeniji, Vincent Bosch, Richard Mawhinney, and Nelson Nieves (Operations); Kathy Thornton-Bias, Dawn Bossman, Norman Laurila, Bonnie Mackay, Seok-Hee Lee, and Ray Martinelli (Retail); LJ Hartman, Fimbar Byam, and Louis Bedard (Security); Nicholas Apps, Elizabeth Graham, Paola Zanzo, Pamela Eisenberg, Lauren Driscoll, and Nicholas Ruiz (Special Programming and Events); Diana Simpson, Lynn Parish, Melanie Monios, Sonya Shrier, and Jean Mary Bongiorno (Visitor Services); Wendy Woon, Pablo Helguera, Laura Beiles, Elizabeth Margulies, and Sara Bodinson (Education).

For their interest and support, thanks to the Film Committee: Ted Sann, Chairperson; Ken Kuchin, Vice Chairperson; Celeste Bartos, Chairperson Emerita; Gregory Todd Allen, George Gund, Taylor Hackford, Drue Heinz, Barbara Jakobson, Jason Janego, Sydie Lansing, Jo Carole Lauder, Susan Lyne, Renville McMann, Jennifer McSweeney, Robert B. Menschel, Si Newhouse, Jr., James Niven, Barbara Pine, Charles Prince, David Rockefeller, Jr., Anna Deavere Smith, Jeremy Smith, and David Stenn; and the esteemed Jerry I. Speyer, Chairman, Board of Trustees and Marie-Josée Kravis, President, Board of Trustees.

Finally, the exhibition benefited from the company of inestimable colleagues in the Department of Film: Sally Berger, Kitty Cleary, Clay Farland, Andy Haas, Jenny He, Jytte Jensen, Laurence Kardish, Mary Keene, Nancy Lukacinsky, Anne Morra, Justin Rigby, Josh Siegel, Charles Silver, Katie Trainor, Pierre Vaz, Arthur Wehrhahn, John Weidner, and Peter Williamson; our resourceful interns, led by Ryan Silveira and Nina Cochran; and in particular, Sean Egan, our Producer of Film Exhibitions and Projects, and Barbara London in the Department of Media and Performance Art.

Major support for the exhibition is provided by MoMA's Wallis Annenberg Fund for Innovation in Contemporary Art through the Annenberg Foundation.

Ron Magliozzi
Associate Curator, Department of Film

Ron Magliozzi

THE MANIC DEPARTMENT STORE

New Perspectives on the Quay Brothers

Sometimes it shocks us how few references people have to the literature and music that has driven us . . . . It makes us feel elitist by default, which is not what we intend. We would rather our films were treated like department stores—admittedly manic department stores—in which one can take a lift to whatever level one wants.

THE QUAY BROTHERS, 1986[1]

It is gratifying to report, right at the start, that the reputed inaccessibility of the Quay Brothers' work is a myth. The challenge of deciphering meaning and narrative in the roughly thirty theatrical shorts and two features that the filmmakers have produced since 1979 is real indeed, a characteristic of their work that they adopted on principle when they were still students. Interpreters of their stop-motion puppet films, such as the defining *Street of Crocodiles* (1986), have described them as alchemists, with the mystifying ability to turn the "degraded reality" of discarded doll parts, screws, string, and metal filings into profoundly expressive characters, and as metaphysicians, whose choreography of objects and camera movement in space is key to understanding their uncanny sense of being. And as Surrealists—although the twins disclaim the label—who stage playful, perplexing, life-and-death scenarios within wondrous, handmade sets and across dreamlike landscapes. The Quay Brothers themselves, valuing their independence from the culture of commercial cinema, identify most comfortably with those alienated from their age, like the writers Bruno Schulz, Robert Walser, and Franz Kafka, whom they have favored in their work, and with genuinely obsessive personalities like Emma Hauck and Adolf Wölfli, who created from behind hospital and prison walls.

To the degree that they have controlled others' access to the full record of their creative lives, including fifteen years working primarily as graphic illustrators, the Quay Brothers have further confounded understanding of their work. A double self-portrait as gnomish Mennonites may be a clue to the spirit of play that motivates them, as might the multiple ways in which the identical twins Stephen and Timothy have signed their work: Brothers Quay, Gebr. Quaij, Stíofáin Valtair MacAae. Or for that matter, their studio name, KonincK, chosen for its typographical symmetry from the label of a Belgian beer. As much as they welcome scholarly analysis, for some time they resisted full disclosure by spreading the fanciful report that all their early films before *Nocturna Artificialia: Those Who Desire Without End* (1979) had been lost.[2] Such strategies have served to maintain the privacy that has nourished the solipsistic nature of their collaborative practice—working alone together nearly every day—for over forty years. They have also effectively limited the revealing connections that might be made between their personal history and the various mediums and genres in which they've worked.

As illustrators, stage designers, and film-makers in a range of genres, the Quays have penetrated many fields of visual expression for a number of different audiences, from avant-garde cinema and opera to publication art and television advertising. Looking at their artistic endeavors as a whole, in the context of fresh biographical information and new evidence of their creativity, provides insight into the roots of their imagination and illuminates a number of essential Quay themes and motifs.

The Quay Brothers were born in 1947 in Norristown, Pennsylvania, a borough fifteen miles northwest of Philadelphia on the Schuylkill River. Once a manufacturing center for "tacks, wire, screws, boilers, bolts, silos, tanks, iron, hosiery, knitting machines, under-wear, shirts, lumber and milling machinery," by the 1950s it was no longer an industrial hub but remained the center of social life for the surrounding rural area.[3] Their father was a first-class machinist; their mother—to whom the twins bear an uncanny physical resemblance—was a home-maker with a talent for figure skating. Tall, sound of body, and agile, the twins considered sports as a life option. In the Mist (c. 1969), one of their amateur films, is a revealing self-portrait of the athletic teenagers, in oversized paper masks, performing a series of comic running and cycling stunts on grass and in a vacant tennis court. A celebration of their "twin-ness," it displays some of the avant-garde imagery that appears in later work: the flat, cut-out paper face they give their composer doll in Leoš Janáček: Intimate Excursions (1983), the vacant, surreal landscape that introduces In Absentia (2000), and the mystifying, rootless trees that suggest the sleep-induced fairy-tale world of The Comb [From the Museums of Sleep] (1990).

One influence on the brothers' choice of art over sport may be found in their exposure to the thriving culture of the local flea markets: suburban "cabinets of curiosity" stocked with the kind of dusty, decaying objects redolent with textures, the call to touch, and secret past lives that would become the stuff of their films. Later, on Portobello Road in London, they encountered a similar milieu: "you find these dolls' heads in a market . . . you live with these things . . . you dream yourself into them."[4] They described their search for artistic inspiration in similar terms: "At worst we think of ourselves as rummaging for lost or obscure foot-notes in half-forgotten alleys of music and literature."[5]

The twins' "facility for drawing"[6] was encouraged by their family. At home, snowy pastoral landscapes of a red barn at different distances were hung side by side, coincidentally suggesting a cinema tracking shot. Stark countryside landscapes dotted with trees appeared commonly in their youthful drawings, often with elements of telling human interest, as in Bicycle Course for Aspiring Amputees (1969) and Fantasy-Penalty for Missed Goal (c.1968). The Quays later remarked that the only "residue" of life in Pennsylvania to affect their work was "the forest and the animals."[7] But it was their art teacher's introduction to illustrator and naturalist Rudolf Freund (1915–1969), who lived twenty miles away in Collegeville, Pennsylvania, that transformed the twins' sense of the world and art.[8] Renowned for his Scientific American covers and his art for Time-Life, Freund had been thinking of a school for illustrators on his farm.[9] He allowed the twins to observe him at his easel and to study what they described as "the kingdom of animals and insects" in his library.[10] The ecological subtext in a number of the Quays' films may be traced to Freund's influence, as some of his assignments, such as the Scientific American cover illustrations Mouse in a Metabolism Cage (November 1956) and Chicken Factory (July 1966), called for the illustration of darker themes. The twins were impressed by Freund's meticulous anatomical research and the luminescent detail in his lifelike art. Having watched him working on the Scientific American cover image Ecological Chemistry (fig. 1, February 1969), a painting of a blue jay choosing between identical living and dead butterflies, they later described the experience as "one of those crucial revelatory moments when something painted was so powerfully tactile."[11] Their experiences with Freund fathered many of the twins' aesthetic principles and provided a model for their consuming work ethic. Expressing the depth of their respect years later, they favorably compared "the care, the patience, the craftsmanship and caliber" of Freund's scientific illustration to the "serious illustration" of "Bonnard, Dulac, Redon, Rackham etc."[12]

In 1965, at the age of eighteen, the Quay Brothers began seven years of study to become illustrators, graduating from the Philadelphia College of Art (PCA) in 1969 and London's Royal College of Art (RCA) in 1972. During this period, two fateful encounters introduced them to the visual language and European subjects they would quickly adopt, and to the medium of film they would

Fig. 1 Rudolf Freund. *"Ecological Chemistry" (Blue Jay and Butterflies)*, cover for *Scientific American*, February 1969. U.S.A. 11 ½ × 8 ⅜" (29.2 × 21.3 cm). The Museum of Modern Art, New York

Fig. 2 Roman Cieslewicz (French, born Poland. 1930–1996). *Katastrofa*. 1961. Poland. Film poster, 33 ⅛ × 23 ³⁄₁₆" (84.1 × 58.9 cm). The Museum of Modern Art, New York

Fig. 3 *Watermark. Joseph Brodsky.* c. 1983–1984. UK. Collage, 11 × 7 ¾" (27.9 × 19.7 cm). QBFZ Collection

eventually take up. It wasn't simply the radical design of the Polish posters that they came upon by chance in an exhibition at the PCA, or the posters' revelation of a foreign world of European opera, drama, music, and cinema that irresistibly attracted them—it was the fact that the posters spoke so freely of their subjects, as if consuming them.[13] The grotesque, surreal, lyrical, and witty work of Roman Cieślewicz (1930–1996), Wojciech Fangor (1922–), Jan Lenica (1928–2001), Franciszek Starowieyski (1930–2009), Henryk Tomaszewski (1914–2005), Wojciech Zamecznik (1923–), and Bronislaw Zelek (1935–) was illustration art with the courage to be strange and ambiguous. If one compares the cityscape motif in Cieślewicz's poster *Katastrofa* (fig. 2, 1961) to the Quays' *Duet Emmo* album cover (1983) and to their art for Joseph Brodsky's *Watermark* (fig. 3, c. 1983–84), the influence is apparent; it may also be detected in the maps and visual textures of *Street of Crocodiles*. The Quays' first professional job came shortly after, in their last year at the PCA: the design of an album cover for American rock band Blood, Sweat & Tears in 1968. Already committed to the Polish poster aesthetic, they submitted a collage of the group standing headless in a field. To their chagrin, Columbia Records responded by "pasting" heads onto their illustration.

Compounding the impact of the Polish avant-garde, the cinema further matured the Quays' aesthetic. They credit Luis Buñuel's *Un Chien Andalou* (1929) as the first film to seriously impress them,[14] as attested by a drawing from their RCA days, which pictures male torsos tattooed with the words *Un Chien Andalou* and *L'Age d'or*, the title of a second Buñuel film (1930). However, it is the experimental shorts of Walerian Borowczyk (1923–2006) and Jan Lenica, which the Quays describe as "animation at its most intense, mysterious and metaphoric,"[15] that most explicitly point the way to the films they would make themselves.[16] The mix of collage, stop-motion, live-action, and trick effects combined with eroticism and weighty subjects would become a Quay signature. The stop-motion reassembly of exploded household items in Borowczyk's *Renaissance* (1963) speaks to the Quays' fascination with the drama of real objects. In his Holocaust allegory *Jeux des Anges* (1964), camera movement and sound impart meaning to drawings of dismemberment. *Une Collection Particulière* (1973), Borowczyk's study of nineteenth-century pornographic devices, is a model for the Quays' museum documentaries *The Phantom Museum* (2003), *Inventorium of Traces* (2009), and *Through the Weeping Glass* (2011).[17] With *Goto L'île d'Amour*, a 1971 collage titled after Borowczyk's first feature, they visualized an extended narrative for the film.[18] As they explained the influence in 1973: "We both draw too much from cinema and pretend that when we are illustrating, we are really animating—composing films with musique [*sic*] only back into still pictures."[19]

In an RCA student publication to which the Quays contributed—along with illustrators Eduardo Paolozzi, Andrzej Klimowski, and Stewart Mackinnon, who eventually made films as well—the effect of the group's exposure to avant-garde image-making was stated defiantly by Mackinnon: "true expression conceals what it exhibits . . . an image, an allegory, a form disguising what it means to reveal, has more meaning than the enlightenment brought about by words or their analysis."[20] The Quays' student films demonstrated their commitment to this manifesto. Each is a tragic allegory, shy of narrative clarity, with enticing hints at twin-ness and veiled autobiography. *Der Loop Der Loop* (1971), *Il Duetto* (1971), *Palais en Flammes* (1972), and an uncompleted de Sade project were clearly the work of illustrators: paper cut-out animation based on ideas begun as drawings. When the Quays made them, illustration was still the career they were set to pursue.

Returning to the United States in 1973, they described a range of simmering influences, ". . . from *Alice in Wonderland* to Kafka's *In Der Strafkolonie* to Rudolf Freund's scientific illustrations for Time-Life. From a film version of Knut Hamsun's *Hunger* to the music of Debussy's for Maeterlinck's *Pelléas et Mélisande*; from Nino Rota's film music for Fellini to Giovanni Fusco's . . . for Antonioni and Maurice Jarre's . . . for Franju. From the self-portraits of Ensor, Bonnard and van Gogh to the autobiographies of Truffaut, Céline, Vigo, Skolimowski. From Resnais' *Nuit et Brouillard* to Marker's *La Jetée*. From de Sade, to Kraft-Ebbing to Buñuel."[21] But over the next six years in Philadelphia and Amsterdam their illustration work was sporadic and unfulfilling: filler for the *New York Times* music review; a black drawing titled "*I Am an Epileptic*" for the *Philadelphia Inquirer*; book covers for suspense and science-fiction novels; and suitably gothic drawings on surgery and cattle mutilation for Hugh Hefner's men's magazines.[22] Their most prestigious work

in the United States was for the Anthony Burgess novel *A Clockwork Testament or Enderby's End* (1975), a dozen black-and-white drawings of the title character in stages of disintegration. Illustrator Andrzej Klimowski remarked sympathetically that "[this] series of portraits . . . will always remain distant . . . can only remain impenetrable despite all signs of introspection."[23] The Quays' most sustained work as illustrators was the series of covers done for the Dutch and British editions of authors Louis-Ferdinand Céline and Italo Calvino, featuring variations of the figurative "extinct anatomies" and *noir* graphics that would surface most expressively in their films.

Disappointments aside, throughout this period the twins experimented with graphics and nurtured their growing enthusiasm for avant-garde drama and music through hypothetical designs for posters, books, and record albums. This "fictitious" work included gymnastic autoerotica for *Mishima* (c. 1971), tortured anatomy studies for *Ul Abnormalna* (c. 1981–82), and several *Enzyklopedie der Modernen Kriminalistik* credited to obscure nineteenth-century criminologists; faux theater posters for the work of German-language playwrights, such as Thomas Bernard's *Der Ignorant und der Wahnsinnige* (c. 1981–82), Peter Handke's *Kaspar* (n.d.), Friedrich Dürrenmatt's *Die Physiker* (c. 1981–82), and Hartmut Lange's *Der Hundsprozess* (n.d.), in which dog heads are attached to decapitated bodies. They also made a *Portrait of Composer Gesualdo* (c. 1976), known for his highly expressive sacred music and for having murdered his adulterous wife and her lover in 1590. In 1981, two years into their professional filmmaking career, the twins were still identified primarily as graphic artists, appearing in the "Radical Illustrators" issue of the British *Illustrators* magazine, among a fellowship of others whose styles, from Sue Coe's neo-expressionism to Terry Dowling's anticommercial proto-punk, reflected various degrees of militancy against the mainstream.[24]

Whatever militancy the Quays felt, they expressed their frustrations most profoundly in private, at the easel, with illustration "reserved in deep shadow (the works . . . we put ourselves into)."[25] In a series of more than a dozen pieces called The Black Drawings (c. 1970s) they defined the visual palette of their future films, creating an *ur*-text that they would return to as well in opera and ballet settings such as those for *Mazeppa* (1991)

13

and *The Sandman* (2000). Titled with obscure references to French wine, electroshock, sports, Holocaust history, Kafka, Céline,[26] and their own travels in Europe, the drawings are *noir* set pieces, each with the requisite blend of angst, sex, and violence; they read like crime scenes glimpsed from a passing tram. The earliest puppet films, *Nocturna Artificialia* and the Kafka adaptation *Ein Brudermord* (1980), created with producer Keith Griffiths, come directly from the drawings.[27] The influence is still strong in the brothers' *film noir* reading of Stanisław Lem's *Maska* (2010). The black may derive from illustration—the intaglio technique that the twins had always admired[28]—but the figurative use of suspended gestures and "privileged point of view" is cinematic.[29] The Black Drawings mark the point at which the twins were ready to step away from illustration and begin to identify themselves as the poets of gesture and alienation they would remain in every medium they touched.

In the 1980s graphic art became a sidebar as the Quays gradually turned to filmmaking fulltime, but they brought to the moving image significant visual motifs initially explored on paper. The elegant line and lettering of calligraphy is an enduring element in their work, from their business cards and book and album covers to the wrought-iron calligraphy of their studio logo, their posters, and the credit sequences in their films. It is celebrated in *The Calligrapher* (1991), memorialized in *In Absentia*,[30] and figures significantly in the design of their sets for *The Cabinet of Jan Švankmajer* (1984), *This Unnameable Little Broom* (1985), *Rehearsals for Extinct Anatomies* (1987), and the music video *Long Way Down* (1992).[31] Calligraphy's lyrical, sweeping gesture and elegant symmetry map movement across the page, *musicalizing* space, the way the movement of the camera, lighting, objects, and performers are used in the Quays' films. The notion of calligraphy extends to the choreographic quality of their films, which, like music, often serves as an "unwritten scenario" of gestures. No wonder their ballet films *Duet* (1999), a return to the theme of twin-ness, and *The Sandman* (2000), which revisits the expressionism of *The Comb*, are so masterful. Recognizing this motivating principle is essential to appreciating their films, be it the choreographed decapitation of the hero in *Street of Crocodiles* or the uncanny *pas de deux* of mannequin and rabbit in *Stille Nacht II: Are We Still Married?* (1992).

Scholars have noted the connection between the themes of "interior and exterior space" and "closure and exploration" in the Quays' films; these motifs are present in their two-dimensional work as well.[32] Rural landscapes are the subject of many of their early paintings (*The Painted Bird*, 1967), albums (*Blood, Sweat & Tears*, 1968; *Mozart Violin Concerto No. 2*, c. 1973), and books (the Calvino series), as well as the more theatrically inclined Black Drawings. Here, as in films like *In Absentia* and *The Comb*, these are ill-defined places, without sunshine—closer to the existential "dust-breeding" ground of Duchamp and Man Ray's *Élevage de Poussière* than the bright edgy landscapes of Tanguy or Dalí.[33] Complementing the Quays' depictions of exteriors, a number of early drawings—including one titled *Kafka's The Dream* (1970)—feature views from inside, with glimpses out through open doorways and windows. What on paper resemble static stage settings on film become claustrophobic interiors, where inscrutable dramas play out. The beloved Pennsylvania woods become metaphorical furniture—reduced to fetishized pine cones and wood grain in *Stille Nacht III: Tales from Vienna Woods* (1992) and the commercial *Wonderwood* (2010)—or moved indoors, as the forest invades the composer's room in *Leoš Janáček: Intimate Excursions*. The troubled explorations that occur through rooms and streets in *Street of Crocodiles* and *Rehearsals for Extinct Anatomies* are allegories for the chaos of the human condition. Quay protagonists exist inside hermetic, unstable spaces, each with a secret history, populated with the fertile refuse of flea markets. Outside, there may be a landscape of dream (*The Comb*) or a view of the void (*This Unnameable Little Broom*).

In recent years the Quays have replicated their visionary rooms for gallery display as the boxes of *Dormitorium* (2006) and a peephole installation, *Coffin of a Servant's Journey* (2007).[34] Again, they adapted their challenging aesthetic to a new medium, as they have previously done for classical and avant-garde drama, opera, ballet, site-specific performance, cinema, commercial television, and music video.[35] In the process, they have added to the surprising variety of options available to viewers willing to enter the Quay Brothers' "department store" and open themselves to uncertainty and the experience of strange new perspectives.

NOTES

1 Chris Petit, "Picked-up Pieces," interview with the Quay Brothers, *Monthly Film Bulletin* 53 no. 629 (June 1986):164–65. Note that in virtually all interviews with the Quays, including this one, quotes are attributed to both brothers rather than either one individually.

2 Hammond, Paul, "In Quay Animation," *Afterimage* 13 (Autumn 1987):66–67.

3 "Norristown, Pennsylvania," Wikipedia. http://en.wikipedia.org/wiki/Norristown,_Pennsylvania. In the 1940s, Norristown had a population of roughly 40,000; it is now approximately 32,000.

4 Kim Newman, "The doll's house," interview, *City Limits* (September 25, 1986):n.p. Museum of Modern Art, Film Study Center clipping file, Quay Brothers. In the interview for this London magazine, the Quays misidentified the Portobello Road market as Finchley Road, an error they corrected in an email to the author on February 23, 2012.

5 Chris Petit, "Picked-Up Pieces."

6 "The Quay Brothers' Perifere Blik" [Peripheral Vision], on-camera interview for the television program *Ziggurat*, BRTN (Belgian Television), July 1996.

7 Teddy Jamieson, "Ten Questions for the Brothers Quay," *Herald Scotland* June 22, 2010. http://www.heraldscotland.com/arts-ents/edinburgh-film-festival/ten-questions-for-the-brothers-quay-1.1036524

8 Freund lived in Collegeville until an aneurism caused his sudden death at 54, shortly after the Quays entered the Royal Academy of Art. Freund illustrated more than thirty books and nature guides, including the Time Inc. Life Nature Library series, and created eighteen *Scientific American* covers from 1954 to 1969. A frequent contributor to *Life* magazine, his "Mythical Monsters" illustrations in the April 23, 1951, issue suggest that he would have been successful as a fantasy illustrator. As a naturalist, he was one of the first to explore the Galápagos Islands and later, with his wife Susan, the jungles of Suriname in South America in 1961, returning with specimens now held by the Yale Peabody Museum of Natural History.

9 Email to the author from Susan Freund Borden, November 7, 2011.

10 Email from the Quay Brothers to Sandy Borden, November 5, 2011.

11 Ibid.

12 Quay Brothers, "The Quay Twins in America," *ARK* 51, Royal College of Art, London (Summer 1973):n.p. Italics in original.

13 *Polish Poster Art*, presented April 1–27, 1967, at the Philadelphia College of Art.

14 Jamieson, "Ten Questions," *Herald Scotland*.

15 Julian Petley, "Puppet masters," interview, *The Guardian* (London), September 25, 1986. Museum of Modern Art, Film Study Center clipping file, Quay Brothers.

16 The Quay Brothers are often paired with Czech Surrealist Jan Švankmajer, the subject of the 1984 documentary *The Cabinet of Jan Švankmajer*, to which they contributed an animation sequence that was later excerpted as a stand-alone short film of the same title. But the Quays discredit Švankmajer's direct influence in this period because they had not as yet encountered his work. Instead, the Quays much admired the Borowczyk-Lenica collaboration *Dom* (1958) and Lenica's *Labyrinth* (1961), and also acknowledge the influence of Soviet animator Yuri Norstein.

17 The Quays' music-box device *Lacrimi Christi*, created for their feature film *The Piano Tuner of Earthquakes* (2005) and included in the touring exhibition of their film decors that began in 2006, is an unspoken tribute to the flycatcher contraption that Borowczyk designed as a prop for his 1969 feature film, *Goto L'Ile d'Amour*.

18 Daniel Bird. "The Ghost of Goto: Walerian Borowczyk Remembered." *Vertigo*, 3:1 (Spring 2006): 57–59.

19 Quay Brothers, "The Quay Twins in America."

20 Stewart Mackinnon, "Manifesto," *ARK* 51, Royal College of Art (1973):n.p.

21 Quay Brothers, "The Quay Twins in America."

22 "The Night Surgeon, fiction by Robert Chatain," *Playboy* 20: 11 (November 1973):96–97; "On the Trail of the Night Surgeons by Ed Sanders," *Oui* 6: 5 (May 1977):78–79.

23 "The Work of Stephen and Timothy Quaij," unidentified Soviet film publication, c. 1986. Museum of Modern Art, Film Study Center clipping file, Quay Brothers.

24 "Koninck, Londyn: The Brothers Quay," *Illustrators* (U.K.) 38 (1981), edited by George Snow and Robert Mason. Also featured in the issue: Edward Bell, Georgeanne Deen, Catherine Denvir, Blair Drawson, Robert Ellis, Carolyn Gowdy, Anne Howeson, Rod Judkins, Andrzej Klimowski, Stewart Mackinnon, Shinro Ohtake, Ian Pollock, Liz Pyle, Sol Robbins, Christine Roche, and Jake Tilson.

25 Quay Brothers, "The Quay Twins in America."

26 Especially provocative are the sinister references to Céline's anti-Semitic texts, *Bagatelles pour un Massacre* (1937) and *L'Ecole des Cadavres* (1938).

27 British-born Keith Griffiths (1947–) met the Quays at the Royal College of Art in London, where he was studying film. He soon became a close friend, traveling companion, and in 1979 co-founder of their Koninck Studios. As an executive at the British Film Institute Production Board in the early 1980s, he was instrumental in the Quays' transition from illustration to film, and eventually shepherded most of their best-known work to the screen.

28 "We've always liked . . . the intaglio technique because you work out of the black, you make things come from the black instead of creating the black." "The Quay Brothers' Perifere Blik." Intaglio is a printmaking technique in which black ink completely covers an engraved or etched printing plate before being wiped away to reveal the outlines of the artist's drawing beneath.

29 "The Quay Brothers' Perifere Blik."

30 It was the manic calligraphic quality of Emma Hauck's letters that inspired the Quays to create this portrait of psychosis.

31 The Quays have repurposed the miniature decors from their films as gallery exhibition pieces, which have toured since 2006 as the *Dormitorium*. The complete title of *This Unnameable Little Broom* is *Little Songs of the Chief Officer of Hunar Louse, or This Unnameable Little Broom, being a Largely Disguised Reduction of the Epic of Gilgamesh*.

32 See Suzanne H. Buchan, "A Metaphysics of Space: The Quay Brothers' Atmospheric Cosmogonies" in Lois Weinthal, ed., *Toward a New Interior: An Anthology of Interior Design Theory* (New York: Princeton Architectural Press, 2011), 527–45; Jordi Costa, "The Quay Brothers, Explorers of Limbos," in the catalogue for the 2001 Sitges International Film Festival, Sitges, Spain, 43–47.

33 An otherworldly Dadaist collaboration by Man Ray and Marcel Duchamp, *Élevage de Poussière* (1920) is the photographic record of the layer of dust that accumulated on Duchamp's sculpture *The Bride Stripped Bare by Her Bachelors, Even (The Large Glass)* (1915–23) over several months in 1920.

34 The number of boxes in *Dormitorium* has varied with each installation, ranging up to two dozen.

35 The Quays' genre parodies for beer, snack food, and weed-killer reveal a sense of humor that they deny having, as well as their secret life as film buffs. Although commercials traditionally call for artistic compromise, the field has employed the talent of such esteemed filmmakers as Oscar Fischinger, Len Lye, and Alexandre Alexeieff and Claire Parker, whose work bears comparison to the Quays'.

Edwin Carels

THOSE WHO DESIRE WITHOUT END

Animation as "Bachelor Machine"

Cinematographic craftsmen in the best sense of the term, the Quay Brothers carefully conceive and construct their images, manipulating every aspect of cinema's language frame by frame. Despite their often fairytale-like protagonists, what the Quay Brothers conceive are intrinsically experimental films, presenting a disorienting frenzy of audiovisual impulses on screen. Why then venture into such different territory, moving from the darkened film theater to the brightly lit museum?

For the Quay Brothers, the migration of their animations into the realm of the exhibition space may be understood as a logical consequence of their aesthetic ambitions. Since the beginning of their career, they have been collaging together their personal art history from often wildly varying sources. They reanimate forgotten figures and anecdotes, taking their cue from minor footnotes and obscure references. Every film seems to operate like a private museum, or rather obeys the idiosyncratic logic of a household altar: an inscrutable assemblage of relics and memorabilia. Since their debut film *Nocturna Artificialia: Those Who Desire Without End* (1979), the artists have consistently based their work on the creation of box-like sets: miniature exhibitions that are governed by unpredictable dialectics of time and space. Unlike live-action film, animation is essentially about creating an imaginary space, not reproducing an existing one; it is about constructing a unique time regime, not respecting the rhythms of what already exists in front of the camera. The way the Quay Brothers stage the gaze for the viewer is quite different from the rules of traditional cinema, with no systematic coherence in the sightlines or spatial logic to the point-of-view shots.

The Quay Brothers were not trained as filmmakers, but as graphic artists. There is an obvious logic to their gradual move from the graphic to the cinematographic and then the scenographic world, at each step adding another dimension. Yet they have been practicing all these activities concurrently, rather than in consecutive phases. Early in their career they began creating imaginary film posters and inventing cinematic situations, and recently began to exhibit these works under the collective title The Black Drawings.[1] When they started conceiving installations for exhibition spaces in the late 1990s, they had already gained experience by creating stage designs for the opera, theater, and ballet. Regardless of the medium—whether a sheet of paper, a camera frame, or a theater set—the Quay Brothers' approach is essentially that of a choreographer. Taking our sightlines for a walk, they direct our gaze through a scripted movement of objects, light, and shadow. In their films, they orchestrate the movement of bodies (puppets, dancers, actors); in their installation work, it is the viewers' motion that is gently manipulated.

To date, the most widely seen installation project by the Quay Brothers has been *Dormitorium* (2006), comprising two dozen dioramas adapted from their film sets. Behind glass, the collaged, three-dimensional still lifes lose their factual character as props and become Joseph Cornell-like boxes. Lured into their seductive configuration, the viewer becomes instrumentalized, like a humble servant, to complete a job: to activate the space, becoming the animator of graphic whirls, dead objects, and frozen gestures.

The first piece that the Quay Brothers designed to function specifically in a museum context was the enigmatic optical box *Loplop's Nest* (fig. 1, 1997), a large-scale wooden chest on a pedestal.[2] As in their films, they resorted to a wide array of lenses to produce anamorphic distortion, blurring, and a deliberately crammed field of vision, in order to make it impossible to define exactly what the eyes were seeing.[3] With these viewfinders abstracting rather than actually revealing the inner sanctum of their incongruous furniture object, the audience was clearly called upon to activate the space; it was up to the viewer to stretch, bend over, and shuffle from peephole to peephole to catch a glimpse of what was going on inside, and to try to animate the interval between these curious keyframes. For this anachronistic peep show, the Quay Brothers recycled several figures and motifs from their film *Rehearsals for Extinct Anatomies* (1987), continuing to explore graphic ambivalences between two- and three-dimensional representation. *Loplop's Nest* can thus be "read" as a deconstruction of the washed-out white world of *Rehearsals*, although the intertitles added to the peepholes—such as "Everyday Gardening" and "Loplop's Speech—in front of a Magnetised Epidermis"—suggested an entirely different kind of narrative.[4]

In hindsight, the opening sequence of *Street of Crocodiles* (1986) had already announced this important shift in approach, from staging a gaze for the camera to trapping the viewer inside a spatial configuration. When the caretaker of a deserted theater steps on stage and peers into what looks like a mutated mutoscope, instead of inserting a token he drops a spit of saliva in the optic device. This unleashes the objects and puppets locked inside the miniature world. Once liberated from its strings, the puppet in the box echoes the caretaker's behavior and starts exploring, obeying his scopic drive as it impels him through a dilapidated neighborhood where shop windows reflect and multiply. This game of *mise en abyme*—where one image can contain another version of itself, or one universe discloses another—is a favorite strategy for the artists, who continuously hint at peepholes and passages as zones of ambivalence or realms just beyond reach.

The problematization of disembodied sight, of visual experience disconnected from the tactile, is a crucial concern for the Quays. In nearly every film there is an obsessive focus on voyeurist puppets with fixed stares. Through the contrasting interplay of a doll's hollow eyes and its restless hands, of static decors and a frenzied camera, the twin filmmakers metaphorically visualize the tension between monocular and stereoscopic vision, between flatness and depth. More than metaphors, their image manipulation constantly hovers between the optic and the haptic (the illusion of touch through other senses). Their film *The Comb [From the Museums of Sleep]* (fig. 2, 1990) offers the most consistent exploitation of this imaginary quality, inviting us to identify with a pair of hands that, independent of their owner, wander about and caress all sorts of materials. The cinematographic play with camera moves, shifts in focus, and blurring similarly evokes a gentle fetishist's obsession with stroking.

Since they combined their anamorphic fairy-tale excursion of *The Comb* with a more explanatory but no less suggestive documentary (*De Artificialia Perspectiva or Anamorphosis*, 1991), the Quay Brothers have continued to warp the distinction between filmic and museum spaces through a string of commissioned films in which they explore particular collections, typically approaching them through the eyes of a solitary nighttime visitor in a *Wunderkammer*, or cabinet of curiosities.[5] These recent documentaries are no less anamorphic, in the sense that each is made from a radically singular viewpoint, mystifying rather than elucidating. Like their painting predecessors from the Mannerist epoch, the Brothers Quay

Fig. 1 *Loplop's Nest*. 1997. UK. Mixed media.
Commissioned by the Museum Boijmans van
Beuningen. Photograph Tom Haartsen

Fig. 2 *The Comb [From the Museums of Sleep]*.
UK. 1990. Film: 35mm, color, sound, 18 minutes

Fig. 3 *PLEASE SNIFF* (1995) as it appears in
*Institute Benjamenta, or This Dream People
Call Human Life*. UK/Japan/Germany, 1995.
Film: 35mm, black-and-white, sound, 104 minutes

systematically include disorienting signals as ironic commentaries on the notion of "true vision" and "the correct angle."

This subversive play with viewers' positions also recurs in their installation works. In the first versions of *Dormitorium*, which filled complete exhibition spaces, the trajectory through the presentation was explicitly non-linear: at the entrance visitors were obliged to choose between starting from the left side or the right.[6] First, however, they encountered the mysterious double glass dome case *PLEASE SNIFF* (fig. 3, 1995), with its two leather tubes leading to a small pile of white powder inside.[7] Such a curious invitation has its precedents in Marcel Duchamp's famous *Prière de Toucher* (Please Touch, 1947), an exhibition catalogue that featured, on the cover, a shapely foam-rubber breast surrounded by black velvet. It was a typical provocation of the unspoken rules of museum display; throughout his career the French avant-gardist trangressed the codes of the exhibition space. One early work—a 1918 study for the radical masterwork *The Bride Stripped Bare by Her Bachelors, Even (The Large Glass)* (1915-1923)—was a small, purely abstract piece that offered a graphic play of perspectives combined with several types of lenses; Duchamp teasingly titled this *To Be Looked at (from the Other Side of the Glass) with One Eye, Close to, for Almost an Hour*.[8] Precisely because he wanted the image to "happen" in the mind and body of the viewer, Duchamp was fascinated by optical phenomena such as anamorphosis, stereoscopy, the effect of complementary colors, and the dioptrics of lenses.

In traditional optical toys like the thaumatrope, kaleidoscope, zoetrope, and praxinoscope, participation was key to activating the image.[9] The installation work *Coffin of a Servant's Journey* (2007) calls for a similar engagement. As they demonstrate with this incongruous construction—something between a coffin and a peepbox, originally placed in front of an actual historical fireplace[10]— the Brothers Quay operate like media archeologists, seducing us to look back at and into older systems of visual representation, not limiting themselves to a traditional genealogy of the cinema, but probing our fascination for all sorts of optical pleasure.[11] Taking their cue from the nineteenth-century traditions of the diorama, the panorama, and the stereoscope, they cultivate this ghostly paradox of tangibility, activating our memories of the sensation of touch. Indeed, film theoreticians such as Noël Burch have claimed that the original, unspoken ambition of cinema and its precursors had always been to offer much more than a strictly audiovisual experience—aiming instead at "building a haptic space," where attention was paid not only to sight and sound but to physical sensations.[12]

In the central section of *Street of Crocodiles*, we see a stuffed crocodile hovering above the scene. More than a literal paraphrase of Bruno Schulz's eponymous short story, this is clearly a reference to the tradition of the *Wunderkammer*, literally the cabinet of wonders. Before museums assumed a more public and pedagogical role, their Renaissance counterparts were private collections: rooms or cabinets in which the owners displayed their often disparate treasures and taxidermic trophies. In the earliest depictions of such cabinets the crocodile was already a prominent feature, usually hanging from the ceiling.[13] As notions of natural history, geography, antiquity, and anthropology were not yet fixed in distinct categories, *Wunderkammer* were conceived as spaces in which all the ingredients for enlightening amazement were perpetually within arm's reach of the happy few who gained access.[14] Once such cabinets were opened to a larger public, vitrines were introduced as well. Objects were put behind glass, and "look but don't touch" became the first commandment of any museum. With this separation, the tactile was traded for the visual, and experience was replaced by knowledge.[15] Aspirations to "haptic space" notwithstanding, cinema may be considered the ultimate culmination of this development: bringing the whole world in sight, yet never truly within reach.

That sort of sensory interpenetration, however, is precisely what drives the work of the Quay Brothers.[16] In their DVD commentaries for *This Unnameable Little Broom* (1985) and *Street of Crocodiles*, the Quays refer to some curious contraptions in their sets as "bachelor machines," a term Duchamp first coined in 1913 in the process of conceiving his *Large Glass*.[17] "I want to grasp things with the mind the way the penis is grasped by the vagina," he once proclaimed, explaining why he developed much of his work around sexual activity in a mechanized environment. Not coincidentally, Duchamp was among the first artists to embrace animation.[18] The bachelor machine's key function is to keep desire circulating without end. Like no others, the Brothers Quay know how to transform humble materials into suggestive sets, and turn them into erogenous zones.[19] Throughout their career, they have continued to play games with these codes and conventions, inviting their public to become (in Duchamp's terms) "oculist witnesses," caught in a configuration in which there is no longer any opposition between the mechanical and the erotic. This is precisely the power animation holds, to trigger deep sensations through purely technical configurations.

More intuitively than Duchamp, yet no less deliberately, the Quay Brothers remind their audiences that it is always deep down the spectator's body where animation really occurs—where intervals are bridged, parallels cross, and all senses get confused. As intimated by their early film titles, *Der Loop Der Loop* and *Il Duetto* (both 1971), the Brothers Quay have cultivated a unique form of binocular beauty, combining stereoscopic vision with *double entendre* on the screen, on stage, and in the gallery space. They combine and contrast, compose and juxtapose, until—for a fraction of a second—dream and reality, time and space, mind and matter collide into a synesthetic experience that unleashes a desire without end.

NOTES

1 This first occurred within the framework of the large group exhibition *The Reality of the Lowest Rank – A Vision of Central Europe*, which took place in six historical locations in Bruges from October 10, 2010, through January 23, 2011. The exhibition was curated by Luc Tuymans, Tommie Simoens, and the author.

2 This optical box, which no longer exists, was conceived by the Brothers Quay as a prelude to the exhibition *Loplop /re/ presents: the im/pulse to see*, a project curated by the author for the Museum Boijmans van Beuningen in Rotterdam (1997). With the title *Loplop's Nest*, the Quays suggest an imaginary accomodation for Loplop, the birdlike alter ego of Max Ernst, which most often appeared in his collages. The same exhibition concept was reprised in autumn 1998 in the Kunsthal Sint-Pieters in Ghent (Belgium), and the box also traveled to Budapest as part of the *Perspectiva* exhibition (Mùcsarnok/ Kunsthalle, summer 1999). The box was then dismantled, but some elements resurfaced in the *Dormitorium* installation. For a well-illustrated documentation of this lost object, see my essay "Crossing Parallels," published in the artists' magazine *COIL* 9/10 (London: Proboscis, 2000).

3 "Anamorphosis" is a distorted perspective that requires the viewer to use a special device or to occupy a specific vantage point to perceive the image correctly.

4 Other peephole intertitles for *Loplop's Nest* included: "At the Edge of This Forest the Text is Waiting;" "The Interior of Sight;" "The Pull of the North (formerly) Travellers into the Total;" and "Up Yours – the Illustrious Forger of Dreams."

5 These commisioned museum films include *The Phantom Museum: Random Forays Into the Vaults of Sir Henry Wellcome's Medical Collection* (2003) and more recently *Inventorium of Traces* (2009) on Jan Potocki's Castle at Łańcut, Poland, and *Through the Weeping Glass: On the Consolations of Life Everlasting (Limbos and Afterbreezes in the Mütter Museum)* (2011), shot at The College of Physicians, Philadelphia. In their DVD commentaries, the artists indicated that they also consider their *Stille Nacht III* (2003) a pseudo-documentary, suitable for a dubious exhibition like those at The Museum of Jurassic Technology in Los Angeles. At least one other museum film never materialized; it was based on Balthus's painting *The Card Players* (1973), in the collection of the Museum Boijmans van Beuningen in Rotterdam. The script of this film was published under the title "Nightwatch" in *Conjunctions 46. Selected Subversions: Essays on the World at Large* (New York: Bard College, 2006).

6 The *Dormitorium* project was originally produced in Amsterdam by the Holland Festival in 2006. It was co-produced by and reprised during the International Film Festival of Rotterdam in 2007.

7 Originally a prop featured in *Institute Benjamenta*, *PLEASE SNIFF* was turned into an artwork for the exhibition *Loplop /re/presents: the im/ pulse to see* (1997). In their DVD commentaries for the BFI release, the Brothers Quay described the olfactory qualities of the sawdust powder of antlers, referring to the smell of semen.

8 This work is in the collection of The Museum of Modern Art.

9 The thaumatrope, for example, is a disc or card with a picture on each side, attached to two pieces of string; when the strings are twirled rapidly, persistence of vision—the same optical phenomenon that makes motion pictures appear to move—causes the mind to see the two images as one. In the opening scene of *Stille Nacht II: Are We Still Married?* (1991), the Quays offered an illusion similar to that produced by a thaumatrope; on their Loplop box they mounted an even more literal version of the illusion, with the classic motif of a bird and cage merging into a single image.

10 This was initially a site-specific installation conceived for the *Picturehouse* exhibition (2007) at Belsay House, UK. In 2011 the Quays reprised the installation in a similar setting in Bruges, as documented in the catalogue *Luc Tuymans: The Reality of the Lowest Rank – A Vision of Central Europe* (Belgium: Lannoo Publishers, 2011).

11 The Brothers Quay are longtime friends of the media historian Siegfried Zielinski, who situates them in a centuries-old tradition in his book *Deep Time of New Media: Toward an Archeology of Hearing and Seeing by Technical Means* (Cambridge, Massachusetts: MIT Press, 2006). The Brothers Quay designed the cover and chapter headings of Zielinski's *Variantology V: Neapolitan Affairs* (Cologne: Verlag der Buchhandlung Walther König, 2011).

12 Burch steered the debate in this direction with his book *Life to Those Shadows* (Berkeley: University of California Press, 1990).

13 See, for instance, Ferrante Imperato's engraving *Dell'Historia Naturale* of 1599, reputedly the first depiction of a cabinet devoted to natural history.

14 In *The Cabinet of Jan Švankmajer* (1984) the Brothers Quay literally tapped into this tradition.

15 Over the last decade there has been a tendency to reorient museum design as a zone for experiences rather than the display of knowledge. See, for instance, Charlotte Klonk's *Spaces of Experience – Art Gallery Interiors from 1800 to 2000* (New Haven: Yale University Press, 2009).

16 Synesthesia is at the very origin of the Quays' career as puppet filmmakers. During their *flâneries* in the Belgian capital in the 1970s, they discovered their vocation when they wandered across Theater Toone, a puppet theater that not only served cherry beer but had puppets made of cherry wood. In the credits of their debut film *Nocturna Artificialia*, they included a dedication to La Mort Subite, both a type of beer and a bar in Brussels of the same name. For an explanation of these events by the Quay Brothers, see the interview "Quaymation" in *Plateau* 12 no. 1 (1991), a quarterly bulletin of international film animation.

17 Duchamp's concept was first elaborated upon by Michel Carrouges in his book *Les Machines Célibataires* (1954, revised and expanded in 1976) and brought to wider attention by curator Harald Szeemann in his exhibition *Junggesellenmaschinen/Les Machines Célibataires*, which toured eight countries beginning in 1975. In his comparison with Kafka's *Penal Colony*, Carrouges defines the bachelor machine as typically consisting of two parts: "*Chaque machine célibataire est un système d'images composé de deux ensembles égaux et équivalents, un ensemble sexuel et un ensemble mécanique.*" ("Each machine consists of a system of images that are composed in two equal and equivalent units, a sexual and a mechanical unit.")

18 See *Anémic Cinéma* (1926). With this film, Duchamp continued his exploration of impossible dimensions, contrasting verbal with visual puns. Krauss describes this as " . . . an oscillating action of systole and diastole, screwing and unscrewing itself in an obsessional pulsation that could be associated to copulatory movements." Rosalind E. Krauss, *The Optical Unconscious* (Cambridge, Massachusetts: MIT Press, 1993), 96.

19 As chance would have it, *The Large Glass* and *Etant Donnés* (1946-66), Duchamp's two major statements on haptic sensation—the one very abstract, the other complementarily explicit—are to be found a mere fifteen miles from where the Brothers Quay grew up, in the Philadelphia Museum of Art. The Brothers Quay admit that they discovered the importance of Duchamp's oeuvre only later, when in Europe. Email conversation with the author, January 24, 2012.

O N DECIPHERING THE PHARMACIST'S PRESCRIPTION FOR LIP-READING PUPPETS

I am he **HEINRYCHO HOLTZMÜLLERO** who was once real and who now only exists under the glass of a museum vitrine in Nürnberg. They are the letters of an alphabet that I created in 1553[‡1] and the sole remaining example of my existence.

OTHERWISE

I am entirely unknown—even, I am told, beyond Google's cyclopic search engine. The Quay Brothers subsequently hand-traced this very same alphabet for use in one of their films, which, in doing so resurrected the near-dormant

SCHREIBMEISTER

in me. They then proceeded to present me with a sketch for a somewhat curious "prescription" in which I was invited to collaborate. Taking up the challenge, I mischievously wrote only the diacritics of this prescription and left it for them to fill in the rest, for which this is the result:

Sýjÿjwgíllä Fl. Zzžřp

FURTHERMORE, they have called upon me to conduct the following conversation with them. Much preferring the rich-ness of my long, moribund slumber and still wishing to remain distant if not entirely absent, I have nevertheless accepted on one condition: that in divining their pronounced weakness for music, I would suspend and vibrate the twin letters » QQ « to resemble the shimmering aura of glass bells which would sufficiently put them into a compliant state to respond to my questions.

I sit here arraigned in paper, black moleskin and entirely ready to attest to the ingredients that I always insisted upon for the blackest of my own inks, which permitted even the deepest shadows to be glimpsed inside the finest of calligraphic hairlines—this ink having been boiled down surreptitiously from that triumvirate of crushed pearls, the musk of a deer, and the testicles of a fox.

‡1
Heinrich HOLTZMÜLLER
Liber Pervtilis 1553 "Basilea"

HH: So, Gentlemen . . . . here we are—me arriving from the 16TH CENTURY and you already ensconced in the present one. I shall attempt to be the "medium" between M o M A and yourselves and to ferret out with my own curiosity what this title: ON DECIPHERING THE PHARMACIST'S PRESCRIPTION FOR LIP-READING PUPPETS might be, as it is clearly not obtainable anywhere, and furthermore, I can see that the legibility of a prescription still hasn't improved over the centuries.

QQs: Yes . . . in our mind it's more of a teasing inducement for a journey. Not a grand journey but a tiny one . . . . around the circumference of an apple. We're no doubt gently abusing the anticipation that the prescriptive side is courting both a rational illegibility as well as an irrational legibility. Hopefully the intrigued will engage with the ambiguity. And besides, the prescription is only mildly inscrutable and one certainly won't die from it, considering that thousands of people a year reportedly die from misread prescriptions.

HH: But it also quickly indicates that due to the errant scribble of the Doctor, one perhaps could already be hovering on the boundary line of an imaginary or forged death. In that sense the so-called calligraphic abuse is already an escort to the grave.

QQs: Goodness no, we meant the prescription as purely imaginary . . . . but with a purpose. However, we must add that it was by your own example nearly five centuries ago, when you proposed an exercise to your students: how best might the word "God" be typographically set in all its *potentia*. And although we know that no trace of that experiment now exists, we do have an example of your work, which is more like a sound poem in which you created a calligraphic equivalent.[‡2]

HH: It was a little experiment to challenge myself with. I simply wanted to hear not only the rooster crowing but the ambient footsteps, the coughs, the sound of the kiss itself, along with that aura of confusion at the moment of Christ's supreme doubt.

QQs: [Long silence as the twins look at one another before one of them pours another three glasses.] Of course that can have no comparison whatsoever, but it can only remind us of the time we went to the Kierling Sanatorium[‡3] outside Vienna, where Kafka died in 1924. And in that very room of his death, we held up a microphone in 1990 with the sublime hope of hearing a vestige of his voice in that last conversation between Klopstock, Dora Dymant, and himself, but of course it wasn't to be and it was utterly futile. All that was heard was the indiscriminate hum of traffic outside his window. If only the tape recorder could record with a kind of carbon-dating perspective, the original wallpaper might still hold the aural DNA to the sound in that room . . . along with the functional banality of a hearse arriving the following day to take his body away.

HH: Kafka I know only as embodying and defining the sole existence of the letter "K" in the kingdom of the alphabet. All others simply have a lease upon it. However, let's return to this prescription. Of course you're being metaphoric: what you're proposing to the viewer is that the prescription *per se* becomes . . .

QQs: . . . a subtle "magnifying" lens to the imagination.

HH: And even an imaginary prescription is meant to help . . . . . [and smiling] . . . . especially those suffering?

QQs: [nodding] Particularly those suffering in health.

‡2
"Olive Pits Removed from the Garden of Gethsemane"

‡3
Kierling Sanatorium, Austria

HH: Yes . . . . they could be the worst.

QQs: And that this magnification should give you, so to speak, a "listening eye"—one that would allow you to hear the infinitesimal hum inside the lips of the puppet.

HH: In other words a kind of Braille, in the same way that fingertips become eyes?

QQs: Yes . . . and without ever once having to resort to an officially corrective eyeglass prescription!! It was meant to help like an endless adjusting screw. There is an admirable quote by Leonora Carrington where she states that one eye should be simultaneously plunged into the microscope, and the other into a telescope. So here you have the microcosm and the macrocosm in one gesture, and on the camera lens itself is marked the very same focal distinction between extreme close-up and infinity.

HH: There IS something marvelous when the eye is confronted by magnification, because it is offered the unfamiliar as a new delirium. With that in mind, how might this correspond to the realm of puppets?

QQs: Analagously it does makes us think of the Belgian playwright Michel de Ghelderode, [‡4] who wrote for puppets and said that to enter a "cave"—where the marionette performances took place—it was important and necessary "to stoop" down . . . to lower oneself to the scale of the puppets and their universe.

HH: And that is indeed a genuine invitation to humility.

QQs: Because they pull you down to their realm and once you adjust to their horizon, then that seems to become the great measure for their "condition of enchantment."

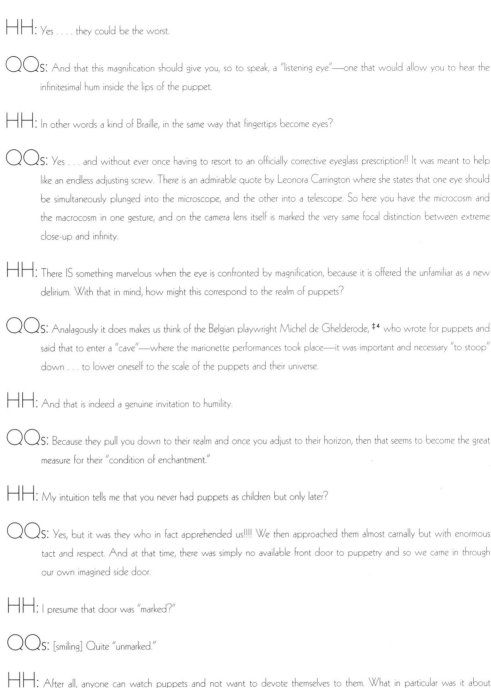

‡4
Michel de Ghelderode

HH: My intuition tells me that you never had puppets as children but only later?

QQs: Yes, but it was they who in fact apprehended us!!!! We then approached them almost carnally but with enormous tact and respect. And at that time, there was simply no available front door to puppetry and so we came in through our own imagined side door.

HH: I presume that door was "marked?"

QQs: [smiling] Quite "unmarked."

HH: After all, anyone can watch puppets and not want to devote themselves to them. What in particular was it about puppets that drew you towards them?

QQs: They seemed to be emissaries from the beyond, able to establish an "otherness" that could distinctly unsettle, and with a purpose. They seemed immensely capable of announcing a halfway world: one caught between an eerie repose and the disturbingly alive and inhabited.

HH: Like the "Mask of the Medusa."

‡5
Toone, *Le Marionnettiste de Bruxelles*, 1956

‡6
Westmalle Trappist beer glass

‡7
Quay Brothers before Café La Mort Subite, Bruxelles, c. 1977

‡8
Théâtre Royal de Marionnettes Toone

QQs: Yes, a mask that aligned itself entirely with the entomological kingdom . . . with laws exclusively their own and this fascinated us enormously. Like the praying mantis, whose movements are at times absolutely motionless, disguised as a leaf gently swaying in the breeze, but then suddenly delivering the most deadly attack on its unsuspecting victim.

HH: Was there any one single epiphany with puppets?

QQs: Bruxelles, 1978, Impasse Schuddeveld, off the Grand Place, when we discovered the celebrated Toone marionettes.‡5 The puppets were riddled with age and had this magnificent patina to them. They were large and heavy and surprisingly crude, operated from above with giant iron rods buried into their heads and strings to manipulate their arms. Their gestures were broad and sweeping, the spoken text was all-important, but there was also a wonderful contamination at work because off to the side, attached to the puppet theater, was a tiny "estaminet" [bar] where you could order those fabulous Belgian beers with all their own unique glassware . . .‡6

HH: Ah! You mean those Krieks [a beer made from cherries] and the Gueuze Lambics and especially those luxuriant Trappist beers made by the monks. And surely you must know the café "La Mort Subite [Sudden Death]?"‡7

QQs: Yes . . . there was no Belgian beer we left untouched in that café, some of which were 10 percent strong. But more importantly, in this atmospheric setting of the Théâtre Royal de Marionnettes Toone,‡8 where literature was indelibly fused with the artisanal side of woodcarving, was born an instant love for puppets, a love hewn from the fruit of their wood and from texts by Michel de Ghelderode, exalted and liquefied by these remarkable beers.

HH: And it's known that the Belgians treat their beers like the French treat their wines.

QQs: And a cuisine to match these beers. And similarly with the puppets: they were taken seriously and had a real legacy. It was at that point that we vowed resolutely to investigate puppets. And since cinema was the one thing that really captured our imagination, we naturally gravitated towards puppet film animation as the form of expression.

HH: But that must have been a sudden leap from an accustomed practice. With that in mind, I noticed some large black and white drawings where an enormous amount of graphite was being expended.

QQs: There was a huge hesitation before arriving at puppet animation. At this time in Philadelphia, mid-1970s, we were totally immersed in European and Central European cinema. These drawings were themselves an elaboration of a much older graphic discipline and, in hindsight now, we realize that they had reached a transition stage as a kind of "failed cinema:" one that desperately begged for the third dimension and a corresponding sound-and-musical universe. But we also realistically knew that no one would ever subsidize a live-action film venture on our part. However, with the realm of puppetry it became the sport of shy boys, where one would be able to work very intimately at a tabletop level and create an entire universe where one could both abolish scale and defy it.

HH: I'm curious about the stories you are proposing to tell with your puppets. They don't seem to be fairy tales *per se* or anything easily recognizable. Why?

QQs: I think initially we were merely trying to establish for ourselves just what puppets might be capable of: what kind of subjectivity, what kind of thaumaturgical murmurings or pathological drifts were possible; and scenographically speaking, what cartographies and "voyages of no return" could occur and what places of the soul might be rendered explorable.

And since we've always maintained a belief in the illogical, the irrational, and the obliqueness of poetry, we didn't think exclusively in terms of "narrative," but also of the parentheses that lay hidden behind the narrative. So it seemed paramount that the narrative not legislate and that it should give to the domain of puppets and objects their own distinct "light" and especially their "shade," so that the subject could pulsate with unknown possibilities—typhoons of splinters at 1/24th of a second.

HH: Indeed, you have given me a palpable glimpse into the *apoteca* of Time fractioned off into tiny frozen sequential moments. And I am made aware at once of the immense temporal and durational slippage that must occur in your work, the dizzying hours inching forward the tiniest sliver of a second in order to capture a mere *spectral* sneeze. And so I ask myself, what is this balm allowing so much concentration?

QQs: Inside every camera such a symbolic apothecary jar should exist!!!! And as well, over every doorway a suspended crocodile! This devotion to preparing a single frame metaphorically brings to mind the poetic notion of Victor Hugo's "velic" point of a boat's sail as that "mysterious point of intersection where all the slight forces along the sails accumulate." These invisible "forces" that fill the image embrace alchemical ones as well.

HH: In mentioning the alchemical, your choice of a writer like Bruno Schulz has meant much for you? To read this author is to be simultaneously drinking one of those great Hungarian *Tokaji Eszencias.*[9]

‡9
Tokaji Eszencias

QQs: Schulz's prose seemed to represent entire kingdoms of what animation "could" be capable of and also a supreme challenge to one's own craft. In particular, the "Treatise on Tailors' Dummies," which introduced Schulz's "metaphysics of form:" that matter was never dead; that lifelessness was only a disguise for hiding unknown forms of life; that it was in a constant state of fermentation and migration. And all this flying under the banner of Schulz's apocryphal 13th "freak" month.

HH: But then music became for you a very vital part of this equation. Even for me, as a calligrapher, it's about generating powerful inner rhythms within the calligraphy. Was it not Tieck who believed that music was the darker, finer language than thought itself, which he found too rational?

‡10
Karlheinz Stockhausen

QQs: For sure, music has unquestionably announced "the" *voyage* for each film and proposed its real secret scenario. This is why we've always demanded to have the music first, and this furthermore explains why the films obey musical laws and not dramaturgical ones. Ideally it is that unforeseen contamination between music and image—where both relinquish their boundaries, where music is "seen" and the image "heard." Dance achieves this eminently, opera as well.

HH: And to the tune of Goethe's beautiful dictum: "architecture is frozen music." Now there are composers whose music simply doesn't have to be rescued by images. Yet your collaboration on *In Absentia* with the composer Karlheinz Stockhausen[10] engraves itself upon me with that single haunting image of a letter written by the insane woman, E.H. [Emma Hauck],[11] to her husband, where she scribbles in pencil: *"Komm, Herzensschatzi Komm"* ("Come, Sweetheart Come") over and over again ad nauseum in an endlessly repeated field of gray overlapping strokes that is so utterly heartbreaking. What I want to know is if there is indeed an invisible boundary between image and music where they become absolutely indistinguishable?

‡11
Emma Hauck, c. 1909

QQs: Perhaps it is simply that immense distance between opposites where Stockhausen's "music of the spheres" is ferociously funnelled and embedded inside the minuscule lead of a pencil point—where even her disembodied fingers, onto which her body seems even more remotely attached, are at the disintegrating mercy of her psychosis. She is utterly and mercilessly subjected to and dominated by the force fields of her illness, which IS the electrifying onslaught of Stockhausen's music. It is through the graphite of her pencil, obsessively worn down millimeter by millimeter, that this victim of paradise ekes out her cosmogony of madness, pencil by pencil, to keep herself sanely insane.

HH: In the setting of texts for books, I was forever limited by the rigorous constraints of readability. Emma Hauck, on the other hand, exploded those margins by the emotive force of her pleas. In that context her obsessively driven handwriting IS a music of cosmic distress, which would be anathema if it ever sat too comfortably inside a book. Far better that it would be served by the cinema.

QQs: As film, the premise for *In Absentia* could not have been scripted on paper, and no flight of any alphabet could have incited words at the level of a scenario for what was inevitably forged directly under the camera with the main actor being "light" itself. The sun's day-to-day trajectory swept mercilessly through her room, engulfing and pulverizing her every effort. An Emily Dickinson in her room immediately came to mind: "Tell all the Truth but tell it slant." This film could only have been achieved using a grammar that was as forcibly mixed as it was invisible. It was not exclusively a live-action film nor was it exclusively an animation film. It was all of these and not only these.

HH: While you were talking just now, I was completely absorbed in watching this very same light straying slowly over our hands and thinking that in our *métier* we work with these hands. But where my hand moves through three-dimensional space, it records that gesture on the page in two dimensions, whilst the puppet animator lodges it into a three-dimensional space which will only accumulate much later on a two dimensional plane. My effect is immediate, yours is suspended.. Nevertheless the element of play is so vital.

‡12
Pages d'examen, Heimatmuseum der Albert Edelmann-Stiftung, Ebnat-Kappel, Switzerland

QQs: One side of us believes that hands left on their own will invite themselves into the amplitude of "play." They are capable of obeying, but as renegades they also think entirely of their own accord and for that reason we follow them willingly. But there is a further spell that happens, that while fabricating the puppets we are constantly absorbing the music for the film, and we are likewise convinced that this music will eventually be transmitted through the fingertips into the puppet or the objects. It becomes a "musicalization" of space, and ultimately all those infinitesimal manipulations of the animator accrue frame by frame to coerce the deadness out of things, giving them their *limbos* and the afterbreezes of a life-beyond-life.

‡13
Page de titre, Coll. S. Haab, Meilen, canton of Zürich, Switzerland

HH: These last words resonate and remind me that my Father in a far-off time was also a calligrapher, trained in the *écoles appenzelloises*‡12 to write and embellish important documents like birth certificates, baptisms, marriages, and death certificates. He was in high demand, and I rarely saw him because he traveled from village to village. And of course worked virtually anonymously, as he chose to hide in the forest of his own calligraphy. Nevertheless, it was in observing him, and even in sleep, that I heard only the sound of quill on parchment and thus became the embodiment of a *calligraphy* in muscle‡13 . . . the wrist eroticised by repeated repetition. And so I'm fascinated how these hypnotic movements bequeath themselves to our souls and wonder if there is something comparable for you.

‡14
Jeane Marie Smith, 1947

QQs: Only recently we discovered a photograph of our Mother at 21,‡14 poised on the tips of her toes in ice skates, and she told us that she was already pregnant with us and yet she carried on skating for a further four months. Not only were we cocooned in a belly that skated daily to the repertoire of classic ballet music, but surely we also heard steel being engraved upon ice beneath us and were already secretly inheriting inside our own skin not only all those compulsory figure eights that she so methodically practiced but also those extended glissades and leaps.

HH: Gentlemen, I can perfectly envision you at four months not only floating inside your *Mother's* waters but floating above these *frozen waters* in her mid-air leaps. Unconsciously already being laid are your first attempts at shaping rhythms in space by being inside them.

QQs: Only later, when as children we were instructed by her to not ever stray outside that first engraved line of the figure eight, did she not inadvertently propose that initial challenge: the perfection of movement within music.

HH: Ah! But then we've come back to dance yet again! But maybe on the other hand, even in your admitted ineptitude at inscribing those perfect figure eights, you were in fact already conceiving those first intimations of animation?

QQs: Hmmmm . . . . . yes, by straying outside the lines. . . . but with just a certain element of skill.

HH: Gentlemen, I see that our glasses are nearly empty, so perhaps we should now return to where we began: your "pharmacist's prescription for lip-reading puppets." What do you expect of your viewers? And especially those who will perhaps not have the perseverance to "decipher" all that lay before them . . . . unlike myself, who is only too content to mine the stratum of unforeseen convergences and the abnormal arrhythmias so well catered to by "imaginary prescriptions."

QQs: . . . . . *IF,* for the most part of some 33 years we have worked at the miniature scale of the tabletop and with puppets, it was in the firm belief that this realm had given the two of us a tiny working door, already slightly ajar but continuously opening onto the marvellous, and onto the reality of unseen worlds and onto, as Cortázar has said, "another order, more secret and less communicable; that the true study of reality did not rest on laws, but the exception to those laws." And that this position in the margins, however imperfect, was ours and is ours; and that this has given us an approach to apprehending life, even in its most fragmentary of forms. To have believed fully in Bruno Schulz's notion of "what is to be done with events that have no place of their own in time; events that have occurred too late or gone un-registered; that there were branch lines of time, somewhat suspect, onto which one could shunt these illegal events." This inherently has become a kind of credo for us, one that we have revered and stubbornly hammered out again and again and at different scales in the work: that one of Kafka's fragmentary diary entries seemed far more evocative and more whole than any of his novels; or, that one of Walser's liminal "micrograms," written on the back of a publisher's rejection slip would not but inspire in us a frenzy of wanting to elaborate and vindicate his imperceptible thresholds and slippages. The further we ventured into a corner the more comfortable the two of us felt in disintegrating it.

‡15

Cartoixa "Scala Dei" from Priorat

HH: Ah! the infinite curve of slowly vanishing perspectives!! Fratelli!! We seem to have finished off two bottles of this ink-black *Cartoixa "Scala Dei"* ["God's Staircase"].‡15 I cannot think what other wine might have led us to such a conclusion, here at the edge of this Carthusian forest!! Come, Fratres! I propose we go for a little walk. We still have much to talk about.

Gathering up the three empty glasses and pulling out a third bottle, arm in arm the three enter the forest. And like one of Walser's seemingly aimless but celebrated strolls, where a path takes you off the beaten track deep inside a museum forest suddenly made mythic by that legacy stretching out before you . . . of trees casting immense shadows from which you will never, ever exist even as a branch, but there beneath your feet are the pine needles bearing the footprints of an Uccello, a Giovanni di Paolo, a Giotto, and the limbs gliding above your head bearing the carved initials of those who have passed before and none dares to reach inside his pocket for a penknife. . . . . Suddenly a breeze rustles through the pines, but they have already vanished deeper into the forest.

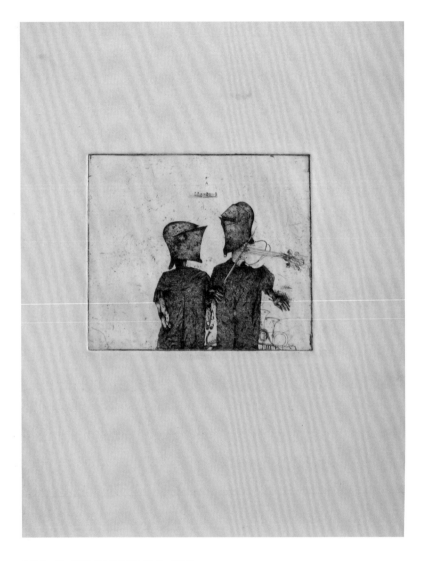

1. *Il Duetto*. 1970. UK. Etching, 15 ¾ × 11 ¼"
(40 × 28.6 cm). QBFZ Collection

3. *Self-Portrait as Mennonites*. 1995. UK.
Photographic print, 12 × 9"
(30.5 × 22.9 cm). QBFZ Collection

2. Untitled (*Tattooed Men*). c. 1970s. UK.
Photolithograph, 9 ¾ × 11" (24.8 × 27.9 cm).
Lydia Hunn Collection

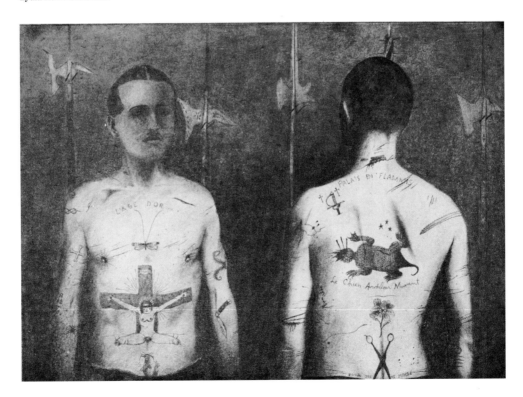

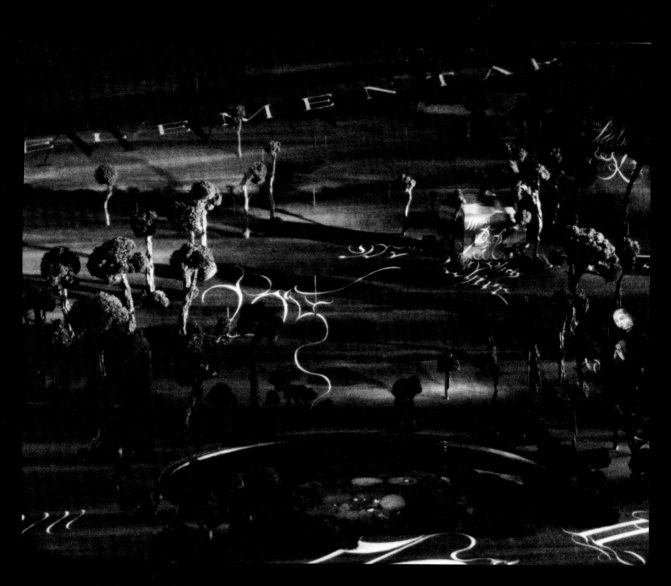

4. *Ex Voto*. 1989. UK/USA.
Film: 35mm, color, sound, 1 minute

6. *Bicycle Course for Aspiring Amputees.*
1969. US. Pencil and oil paint on
illustration board, 7 ½ × 7" (19.1 × 17.8 cm).
QBFZ Collection

5. *Fantasy – Penalty for Missed Goal.*
c 1968. US. Pencil on paper, 10 × 16"
(25.4 × 40.6 cm). QBFZ Collection

7. Poster for *Stille Nacht Dramolet*. 1988.
UK. Mixed media (photograph, tracing paper, ink),
8 ½ × 6" (21.6 × 15.2 cm). QBFZ Collection

8. *Test for The Calligrapher Film Project*. 1991.
UK. Collage on paper, 11 ½ × 8 ⅛" (29.2 × 20.6 cm).
QBFZ Collection

9. *The Calligrapher*, decor for BBC 2 ident.
1991. UK. Wood, fabric, glass, metal,
29 ⅛ × 20 ½ × 19 ¹¹/₁₆" (74 × 52 × 50 cm).
Photograph Robert Barker, Cornell University

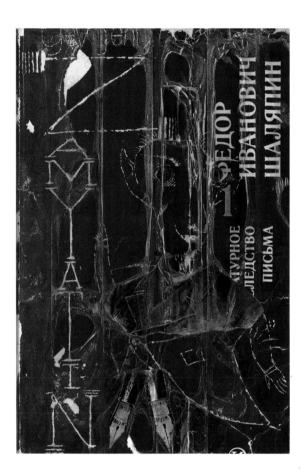

10. Book cover for
Zamyatin. c. 2000. UK.
Collage photo offset,
8 × 5" (20.3 × 12.7 cm).
QBFZ Collection

12. *Serenato in Vano Love Duets*.
c. 1971–72. UK. Pen and ink on
paper, 10 × 7 ½" (25.4 × 19.1 cm).
QBFZ Collection

11. *Hundsproceß.*
Hartmut Lange. c. 1980.
UK. Acrylic paint and
typography, 13 ½ × 9 ¾"
(34.3 × 24.8 cm).
QBFZ Collection

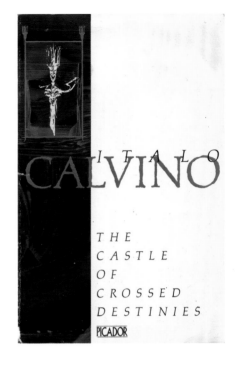

15. Book cover for *The Castle
of Crossed Destinies.*
Italo Calvino. 1978. UK.
Photo offset, 7 ¾ × 5"
(19.7 × 12.7 cm).
QBFZ Collection

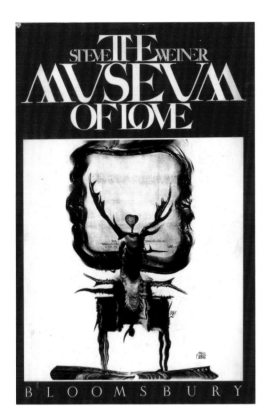

13. Book cover for
The Museum of Love.
Steve Weiner. 1993. UK.
Photo offset, 9 ½ × 6 ¾"
(24.1 × 17.1 cm).
QBFZ Collection

14. Book cover for *Normance.*
Louis-Ferdinand Céline. 1994. UK.
Photo offset, 8 × 5" (20.3 × 12.7 cm).
QBFZ Collection

16. *On the Trail of the Night Surgeons.*
1977. US. Pencil, 16 ¼ × 10 ¾" (41.3 × 27.3 cm).
QBFZ Collection

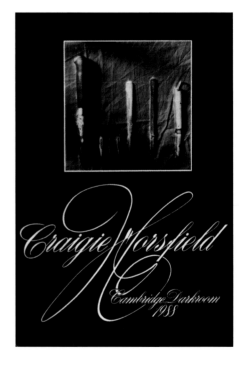

17. Poster for *Craigie Horsfield,*
Cambridge Darkroom. 1988. UK. Photograph
and typography, 8 × 5 ¼" (20.3 × 13.3 cm).
QBFZ Collection

18. *Les Excursions de Mme Broucek.*
1971. UK. Etching, 13 ¾ × 9 ¹⁄₁₆" (34.9 × 23 cm).
QBFZ Collection

19. *Jó Menő Szerelmesek.* c. 1970s. US.
Pencil on paper, 20 ¹⁄₁₆ × 15 ¹⁵⁄₁₆" (51 × 40.5 cm).
QBFZ Collection

20. *A Fratricide by Franz Kafka*. 1970.
UK. Pencil on paper, 8 × 6" (20.3 × 15.2 cm).
QBFZ Collection

21. Scenario image from *Stille Nacht V*. 1991.
UK. Collage on paper, 11 ½ × 6 ½" (29.2 × 16.5 cm).
QBFZ Collection

22. *Coffin of a Servant's Journey.* 2007.
UK. Mixed media, 72 1/16 × 17 11/16 × 63"
(183 × 45 × 160 cm). Photograph Keith Paisley.
QBFZ Collection

23. *Portrait of Composer Gesualdo.* c. 1976.
US. Pencil drawing (photographic copy),
8 × 6" (20.3 × 15.2 cm). QBFZ Collection

24. Program cover for *A Flea in Her Ear.*
George Feydeau. 1989. Old Vic, London. Photo
offset, 8.3 × 3.9" (10 × 21 cm). QBFZ Collection

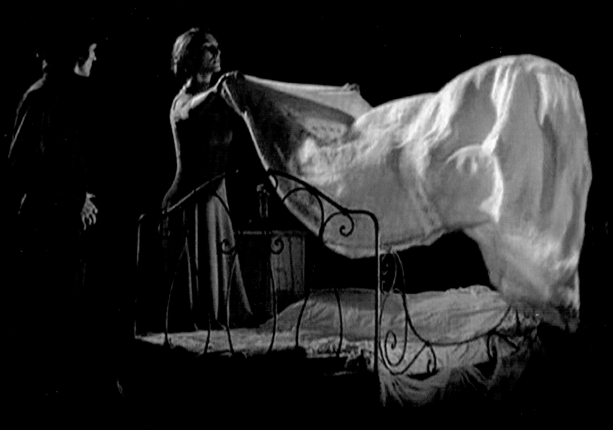

25. *The Sandman*. 2000. UK. Film: Super
16mm, color, sound, 41 minutes

30. *Skips* (K.P. Skips promotional spot). 1988. UK.
Film: 35mm, color, sound, 40 seconds

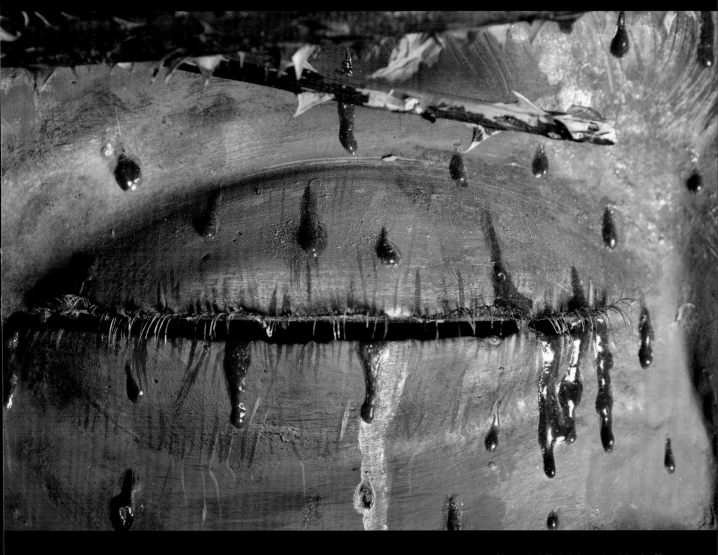

33. *Lacrimi Christi*, decor detail for the film *The Piano Tuner of Earthquakes*. 2005. UK. Wood, fabric, glass, metal, 56 ⁵⁄₁₆ × 30 ¹¹⁄₁₆ × 42 ½" (143 × 78 × 108 cm). Photograph Robert Barker, Cornell University

31. Decor detail for the film *Little Songs of the Chief Officer of Hunar Louse, or This Unnameable Little Broom, being a Largely Disguised Reduction of the Epic of Gilgamesh*. 1985. UK. Balsa wood, metal armature, fabric, 35 ½ × 52 × 37 ¾" (90 × 132 × 96 cm). Photograph Robert Barker, Cornell University

32. *O Inevitable Fatum*, decor detail for the film *Rehearsals for Extinct Anatomies*. 1987. UK. Grapevine, balsa wood, garlic husk, wire, metal, glass eyes, 15 ½ × 16 ½ × 19 ¾" (39 × 41.5 × 50.5 cm). Photograph Robert Barker, Cornell University

34. Untitled (*Ballerina Suspended over the Herd*). c. 1966–1967. US. Pen, ink, acrylic paint, 7 ¾ × 6" (19.7 × 15.2 cm). QBFZ Collection

35. The Phantom Museum: Random Forays into the Vaults of Sir Henry Wellcome's Medical Collection. 2003. UK. Film: 35mm, black-and-white and color, sound, 12 minutes

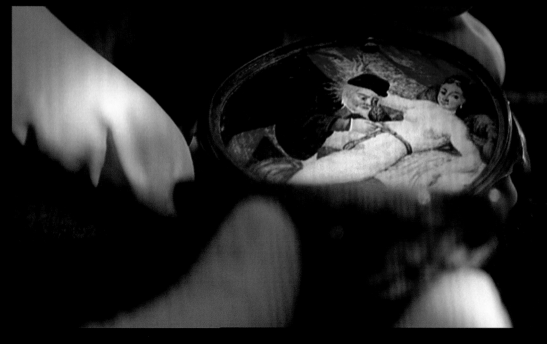

36. *Long Way Down (Look What the Cat Drug In)*. 1992. UK/USA. Film: 35mm, color, sound, 4 minutes

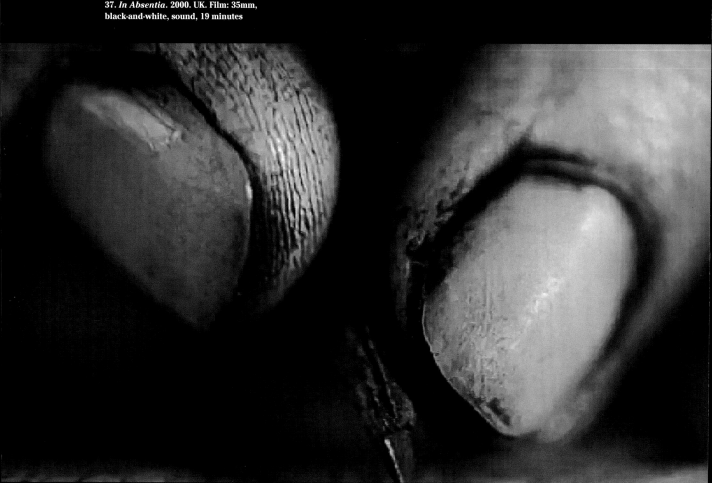

38. *Stille Nacht II: Are We Still Married?* 1992.
UK. Film: 35mm, color, sound, 3 minutes.

39. *They Think They're Alone*, decor for the film *Rehearsals for Extinct Anatomies*. 1987. UK. Wood, fabric, glass, metal, 30 ¹¹⁄₁₆ × 24 ⁷⁄₁₆ × 26 ¾" (78 × 62 × 68 cm). Photograph Robert Barker, Cornell University

40. *The Alchemist of Prague*, decor for the film *The Cabinet of Jan Švankmajer*. 1984. UK. Wood, fabric, glass, and metal, 37 × 29 ⅛ × 29 ⅛" (94 × 74 × 74 cm). Photograph Robert Barker, Cornell University

41. *Tailor's Shop*, decor for the film *Street of Crocodiles*. 1986. UK. Wood, glass, plaster, and fabric, 35 ⁷⁄₁₆ × 26 × 30 ⁵⁄₁₆" (90 × 66 × 77 cm). Photograph Robert Barker, Cornell University

42. *Grand Box*, decor for the film *Street of Crocodiles*. 1986. UK. Wood, glass, plaster, and fabric, 55 ⅛ × 37 ⅜ × 41 ¾" (140 × 95 × 106 cm). Photograph Robert Barker, Cornell University

43. *The Lining of Sleep*, decor for the film
Stille Nacht I. 1988. UK. Wood, glass,
plaster, fabric, and wire wool, 43 $^{11}/_{16}$ × 24 $^{13}/_{16}$ ×
30 $^{11}/_{16}$" (111 × 63 × 78 cm). QBFZ Collection

44. *Kafka's The Dream*. 1970. US.
Pencil on paper, 7 ½ × 7 ½" (19.1 × 19.1 cm).
QBFZ Collection

45. *Anthony Burgess. The Clockwork Testament.*
c. 1974. US. Pencil on paper,
10 ½ × 10 ¼" (26.7 × 26 cm). QBFZ Collection

46. *"I Am an Epileptic."* 1974. US.
Black ink on scratchboard, 12 × 11"
(30.5 × 27.9 cm). QBFZ Collection

47. *Castle to Castle.* c. 1970s.
UK. Pencil on paper, 9 7/16 × 7 1/16"
(24 × 18 cm). QBFZ Collection

56

49. *Ballets sans musique, sans personne, sans rien. L. F. Céline.* c. 1980. UK. Etching, 7 × 5" (17.8 × 12.7 cm). QBFZ Collection

48. Book cover for *Die Tortur, Enzyklopädie der Modernen Kriminalistik. Dr Fritz Helbing.* c.1980. UK. 8 × 5 ¼" (20.3 × 13.3 cm). QBFZ Collection

50. *Mishima.* c. 1971. UK. Pencil and typography, 7 ¼ × 5" (18.4 × 12.7 cm). QBFZ Collection

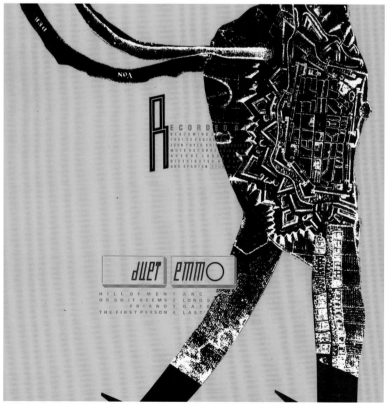

51. *Duet Emmo.* 1983. UK.
Photocopy and collage,
12 ¼ × 12 ¼" (31.1 × 31.1 cm).
QBFZ Collection

52. *Chateau de Labonnécuyère.* c. 1970s.
US. Pencil on paper, 28 ⅜ × 18 ½" (27 × 47 cm).
QBFZ Collection

53. *Lover Practicing Hate.* c. 1970s. US.
Pencil on paper, 30 ⁵⁄₁₆ × 20 ¹⁄₁₆" (77 × 51 cm).
QBFZ Collection

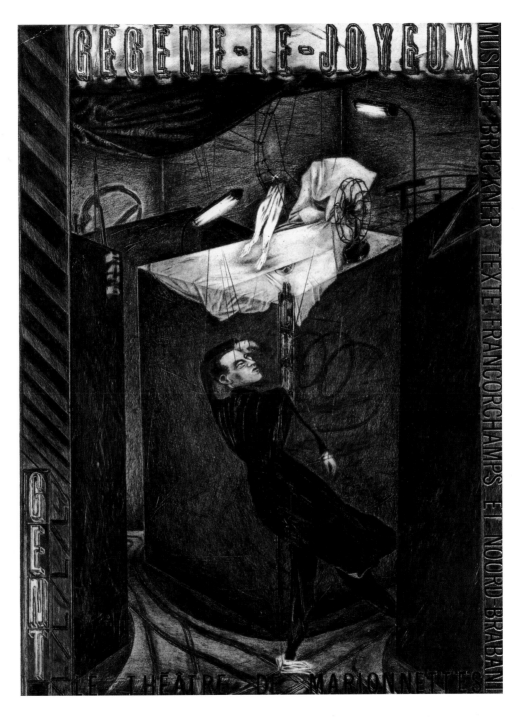

54. *Gégène-Le-Joyeux.* c. 1970s. US.
Pencil on paper, 13 × 9 ⁷⁄₁₆" (33 × 24 cm).
QBFZ Collection

The Metamorphosis. France, 2012 Digital video. Based on a short story by Franz Kafka. For Cité de la Musique, Paris.

Through the Weeping Glass: On the Consolations of Life Everlasting (Limbos & Afterbreezes in the Mütter Museum). USA, 2011. Digital video. For The College of Physicians of Philadelphia.

Bartók Béla: Sonata for Solo Violin. UK, 2011. Digital video. For Chetham's School of Music, Manchester.

Maska. Poland, 2010. Digital video. Based on a short story by Stanisław Lem.

Inventorium of Traces – Jan Potocki at Castle Łańcut. Poland, 2009. Digital video.

Stille Nacht V: Starman, second version. UK, c. 2008-2010. Digital video. Music video with Sabisha.

Muslingauze. UK, c. 2008-2010. Digital video. Music video for D.J. Spooky.

Ubu Roi. UK, 2008. Digital video. Music video projections, series of fifteen, in collaboration with the band Pere Ubu.

Eurydice, She So Beloved. UK, 2007. Digital video. Ballet film with choreographer Kim Brandstrup for Opera North and The Capture Company.

Alice in Not So Wonderland. UK, 2007. Digital video. For Live Earth.

Bruno Schulz, Fragments & Scenes - Sanatorium Under the Sign of the Hourglass. UK, 2006. Digital video. Pilot for feature film.

The Piano Tuner of Earthquakes. Germany/UK/France, 2005. 35mm. Feature film.

The Phantom Museum: Random Forays into the Vaults of Sir Henry Wellcome's Medical Collection. UK, 2003. 35mm. For the Wellcome Trust.

Songs for Dead Children. UK, 2003. Digital video. Collaboration with Steve Martland for the Tate Modern.

Frida (animation sequence). USA/Canada/Mexico, 2002. For the feature-film biography of Frida Kahlo directed by Julie Taymor.

Stille Nacht V: Dog Door. UK, 2001. Digital video. Music video for Sparklehorse.

In Absentia. UK 2000. 35mm.

The Sandman. UK, 2000. Super 16mm. Ballet film choreographed by Will Tuckett.

Duet - Variations for the Convalescence of 'A.' UK, 1999. Super 16mm. Ballet film choreographed by Will Tuckett.

Black Soul Choir. USA, 1996. 35mm/16mm/digital video. Music video for 16 Horsepower, co-directed with David Eugene Edwards.

The Summit. UK, 1995. Mini-DV. In collaboration with performance artists Ralf Ralf.

Institute Benjamenta, or This Dream People Call Human Life. UK/Japan/Germany, 1995. 35mm. Feature film.

Stille Nacht IV: Can't Go Wrong Without You. UK, 1993. 35mm. Music video for His Name is Alive.

Stille Nacht III: Tales from Vienna Woods. UK, 1992. 35mm.

Long Way Down (Look What the Cat Drug In). UK/USA, 1992. 35mm. Music video for Michael Penn.

Stille Nacht II: Are We Still Married? UK, 1992. 35mm. Music video for His Name is Alive.

The Calligrapher, Parts I, II, III. UK, 1991. 35mm.

De Artificiali Perspectiva, or Anamorphosis. UK, 1991. 35mm. Documentary.

The Comb [From the Museums of Sleep]. UK, 1990. 35mm.

Ex Voto. UK/USA, 1989. 35mm.

Stille Nacht: Dramolet. UK/USA, 1988. 35mm. MTV Art Break.

Rehearsals for Extinct Anatomies. UK, 1987. 35mm.

Sledge Hammer. UK, 1986. 35mm. Animated sequences for the Peter Gabriel music video.

Street of Crocodiles. UK, 1986. 35mm.

Little Songs of the Chief Officer of Hunar Louse, or This Unnameable Little Broom, being a Largely Disguised Reduction of the Epic of Gilgamesh. UK, 1985. 16mm.

The Cabinet of Jan Švankmajer. UK, 1984. 16mm.

Leoš Janáček: Intimate Excursions. UK, 1983. 16mm. Documentary.

Igor, The Paris Years Chez Pleyel. UK, 1982. 16mm. Documentary about Igor Stravinsky.

The Eternal Day of Michel De Ghelderode, 1898-1962. UK, 1981. 16mm. Documentary.

Ein Brudermord. UK, 1980. 16mm.

Punch and Judy: Tragical Comedy or Comical Tragedy. UK, 1980. 16mm. Co-directed with Keith Griffiths. Documentary.

The Falls. UK, 1980. The Quay Brothers appear as fictional characters in the Peter Greenaway film.

Nocturna Artificialia: Those Who Desire Without End. UK, 1979. 16mm.

INSTALLATIONS

Coffin of a Servant's Journey. Optical box. 2007, Belsay Hall, Northumberland.

Eurydice, She So Beloved. Optical box. 2007, Leeds Art Gallery, Leeds.

Dormitorium. Decors. 2006, Holland Festival, Amsterdam and touring.

Loplop's Nest. Optical box. 1997, Museum Boijmans van Beuningen, Rotterdam.

STUDENT FILMS

Untitled (travel films). c. 1970s. 8mm.

Frequenzen, Detonation, Stille. USA, c. 1975-76. 16mm.

Venable Lewellyn's Last Waltz. UK, c. 1972. 16mm. Live action.

Palais en Flammes. UK, 1972. 16mm. Paper animation.

Il Duetto. UK, 1971. 16mm. Paper animation.

Der Loop Der Loop. UK, 1971. 16mm. Paper animation.

Pohadka (Fairy Tale). USA/UK, c. 1968-69. 16mm. Paper animation.

Golgatha. USA/UK, c. 1968-69. 16mm. Paper animation.

In the Mist (How Strange Was My Love, Fantasie Part 1). USA, c. 1969. 16mm. Live action.

Muskrat. USA, c. 1967-68. 16mm. Live action.

COMMERCIAL SPOTS

Wonderwood. 2010. Comme des Garçons.

Kinoteka, 1st Polsk Filmfestival ident. 2009. Polish Institute, London.

Mistletoe Kisses, Galaxy. 2007. Mars, Inc.

NHL, Laundromat. 2001. Fox Sports.

NHL, Library. 2001. Fox Sports.

Magnets. 2001. Chili's.

Rice Krispies Treats - Float. 2000. Kellogg's.

Pitney Chairs. 1999. Pitney.

Northern Rock. 1999. Northern Rock.

Mars Celebration. 1998. Mars, Inc.

Fox and Crow. 1998. Badoit.

Lion and Zebra. 1998. Badoit.

Weed Families. 1998. Roundup.

Weeds. 1998. Roundup.

Doritos idents. 1997. Frito-Lay.

The Wooden Box That Collapses (title sequence). 1997. The End.

Lockets Metallica. 1996. Mars, Inc.

Swallow. 1996. Murphy's Irish Stout.

Warriors. 1996. Murphy's Irish Stout.

Brainfreeze. 1995. 7-Eleven Slurpee.

Blue Cross. 1995. Blue Cross Blue Shield Association.

Dolls. 1994. The Partnership for a Drug Free America.

Trees. 1993. Coca-Cola.

Le Bourgeois Gentilhomme (title sequence). 1993. The End.

Fun Touch. 1989. Nikon.

Zenith. 1988. MTV.

MTV ident. 1988. MTV.

BFI ident. 1998. British Film Institute.

Skips. 1988. K.P. Skips.

Dulux. 1987. Dulux.

Walkers Crisps. 1986. Walkers.

Honeywell. 1986. Honeywell Computers.

STAGE AND SITE-SPECFIC PROJECTS

Overworlds & Underworlds. A Leeds Canvas initiative for the 2012 Cultural Olympiad, Leeds. 2012.

I looked back when I reached halfway. 2011. Collaboration with violinist Alina Ibragimova on Béla Bartók's *Sonata for Violin* (1944). Chetham's School of Music/Manchester International Festival, Manchester; Wilton's Music Hall, London.

Bring Me the Head of Ubu Roi. 2008. Projections for Pere Ubu. Queen Elizabeth Hall, London.

Paul Bunyan. 2007. By Benjamin Britten, directed by Nicholas Broadhurst. Theater am Kornmarkt Bregenz/Theater Luzern.

Pinocchio. 2006. By Martin Ward, choreographed and directed by Will Tuckett. Royal Opera House, London.

The Cricket Recovers. 2005. By Richard Ayres, directed by Nicholas Broadhurst. Aldeburgh Festival, Suffolk, and Almeida Opera, London.

The Anatomy of a Storyteller. 2004. Ballet by Kim Brandstrup. Royal Opera House, London.

Death and Resurrection. 2003. By J. S. Bach and Steve Martland, conducted by Sir John Eliot Gardner, Steve Martland. Four short films illustrating Martland's *Street Songs.* Tate Modern and St. Paul's Cathedral, London.

The Wind in the Willows. 2002. Ballet by Will Tuckett. Royal Opera House, London.

The Love For Three Oranges. 1988. By Sergei Prokofiev, directed by Richard Jones. Opera North, Leeds/English National Opera, London.

Queen of Spades. 2001. Ballet by Kim Brandstrup. Les Grands Ballets Canadiens, Montreal.

Baa-Laamsfest. 1999. By Olga Neuwirth, directed by Nicholas Broadhurst. Wiener Festwochen, Vienna.

The Chairs. 1997. By Eugène Ionesco, directed by Simon McBurney. Theatre de Complicité and Royal Court, London and John Golden Theater, New York.

Cupid & Psyche. 1997. Ballet by Kim Brandstrup. Royal Danish Ballet, Copenhagen.

The Hour We Knew Nothing of Each Other. 1996. By Peter Handke. Theater ballet directed by Kim Brandstrup. Malmo Dramatiska Theatre, Sweden.

A Midsummer Night's Dream. 1996. By William Shakespeare, directed by Jonathan Miller. Almeida Theatre, London.

Le Bourgeois Gentilhomme. 1992. By Molière, directed by Richard Jones. Royal National Theatre, London

Mazeppa. 1991. By Pyotr Ilyich Tchaikovsky, directed by Richard Jones. Bregenz Festival/Nederlands Opera

A Flea in Her Ear. 1989. By Georges Feydeau, directed by Richard Jones. Old Vic, London.

Dybbuk. 1988. Ballet by Kim Brandstrup. The Place, London.

SELECTED BIBLIOGRAPHY

Atkinson, Michael. "The Night Countries of the Brothers Quay." *Film Comment* 30: 5 (September–October 1994): 36–44.

Barker, Jennifer M. *The Tactile Eye: Touch and the Cinematic Experience.* Berkeley: University of California Press, 2009.

Buchan, Suzanne. *The Quay Brothers: Into a Metaphysical Playroom.* Minneapolis: University of Minnesota Press, 2011.

Goodeve, Thyrza Nichols, "Dream Team: Thyrza Nichols Goodeve Talks with the Brothers Quay." *Artforum* 34: 8 (April 1996): 82–85, 118, 126.

Habib, André. "Through a Glass Darkly – Interview with the Quay Brothers." *Senses of Cinema* no. 61 (2002). Available online at www.sensesofcinema.com/2002/feature-articles/quay/.

Kitson, Claire. *British Animation: The Channel 4 Factor.* London: Parliament Hill Publishing, 2008.

Klein, Norman M. *The Vatican to Vegas: A History of Special Effects.* New York: The New Press, 2004.

Kleinman, Kent. "Interview with Stephen and Timothy Quay: To Those Who Desire Without End," in *After Taste: Expanded Practice in Interior Design,* ed. Kent Kleinman, Joanna Merwood-Salisbury, and Lois Weinthal. New York: Princeton Architectural Press, 2011.

Le Fanu, Mark. "Modernism, Eccentrism: The Austere Art of Atelier Koninck." *Sight and Sound,* no. 53 (1984): 135–38.

Miller, Tyrus. "'Cut Out from Last Year's Moldering Newspapers:' Bruno Schulz and the Brothers Quay on *The Street of Crocodiles,*" in *Screening the City,* ed. Mark Shiel and Tony Fitzmaurice. London: Verso, 2003.

Quay Brothers. "Ten Unproduced Scenarios." *Conjunctions,* no. 46 (2006): 347–97.

Waisnis, Edward, ed. *Dormitorium: An Exhibition of Film Decors by the Quay Brothers.* Philadelphia: The University of the Arts, 2009.

Weiner, Steve. "The Quay Brothers' *The Epic of Gilgamesh* and the 'metaphysics of obscenity,'" in *A Reader in Animation Studies,* ed. Jayne Pilling. Bloomington: University of Indiana Press, 1998.